WELLSPRING

On the Myth and Source of Culture

ROBERT PLANT ARMSTRONG

WELLSPRING

On the Myth and Source of Culture

UNIVERSITY OF CALIFORNIA PRESS

Berkeley · Los Angeles · London

University of California Press
Berkeley and Los Angeles, California

University of California Press, Ltd.
London, England

ISBN 0-520-02571-7
Library of Congress Catalog Card Number: 73-85781
Printed in the United States of America

In Love and Gratitude

to

Dr. Josie M. Trinkle

Vive Valeque

and

Flora Coffroth Hughes

In Memoriam

Mizpah

Contents

Acknowledgments

The Museum of Cultural History of the University of California at Los Angeles has kindly given permission to reproduce the Sango pedestal in plate 1. The photograph is by Larry Dupont.

Mr. Herbert Baker has given his kind permission to include the kajéguélédia in plate 6. Mr. Baker took the photograph. I wish to thank Mr. George Ellis of the above-mentioned museum for locating this rare piece for me.

The head from Ife which is shown in plate 11 is from the collections of the Department of Antiquities of the Government of Nigeria, specifically from the museum in the Afin of the Oni of Ife. The photograph is by Francis Speed and is reprinted here with the permission of Frank Willett. Dr. Roger Burdé (Roger, Cte de la Burdé) has kindly given his permission to include the bronze pieces shown in plates 22 and 23.

Goya's *Prison Scene*, plate 19, is reproduced in this work through the kindness of The Bowes Museum, Barnard Castle, County Durham. The photograph is from the museum.

All other photographs in this book were made by Warren Eric Frey.

Preface

Sometimes anthropology is little more than the exercise of exotic nit-picking, owing to its origin in a mere phenomenalism which leads many of its field workers to dote upon things and structures. But the end of what I think of as *real anthropology* is in the deep mid-point of human *being* where there is to be found an understanding, an appreciation, and a compassion for man. The study of anthropology ought to ennoble both the student and the studied. One only starts at a consideration of things and structures; after that one dives—or ought to dive—determinedly toward a deep center. The question the anthropologist ought always to ask is: What is the *significance* of what I study? If he cannot provide a persuasive answer to this question, he should abandon the project. I believe the study of man ought to be fraught with meaning for man. This is a primary tenet of humanistic anthropology.

Years ago I began studying art at the "thing" and "function" level. But this was work on the periphery of real anthropology and it did not involve me with man. It kept me busy, but I came to feel I was merely spinning along the rim of the study of man. When I began to slow down I started to think about the work of art—what *manner* of thing is it? I did not find satisfactory answers in the writings of either anthropologists or aestheticians. Anthropologists knew next to nothing about the work of aestheticians who in turn appeared to know nothing at all about the work of anthropologists. Both were too concerned with their disciplines to care about what I regarded as the central question: What is art that man is mindful of it? Anthropologists and philosophers alike in their responses to this question were preoccupied with *meaning*—most anthropologists finding the work's meaning to be identical with its uses, and a number of philosophers finding it to mean that idea or feeling in respect of which it stood as a symbol. But I doubted that art *meant* anything at all. The study of art, I was persuaded, had been obfuscated and subverted by rationalism.

My response, in due time, was *The Affecting Presence: An Essay in Humanistic Anthropology* (University of Illinois Press, 1971). In that book I argued that the work of art is not a function or a symbol, nor anything else, but a living presentation of man's being.

The importance of this to the study of man is this: if one studies art one studies the externalization of man's interiority—an actuality of human experience. This one cannot do by any other means. Art is *man living*. I was concerned with establishing this principle and also with two other problems, the first of which was to identify some of the revealing physical features of the work of art, showing their cultural variability. I wanted to show art as a phenomenon of man writ whole and large. In the second place, I wanted to describe the range of these parameters and to reveal in depth some of the art of particular people. *The Affecting Presence* was intended to present a theory, to show range, and in general terms to focus on a case. I hope others will develop some of its ideas further.

But some months after that book was completed, I grew aware that I had taken but a turn or two on a spring which when fully wound would drive the engine of a whole theory. There was a considerable way yet to go. Every conclusion is but a resting point. So I retarded my momentum a bit more and, like an object in slowing orbit, I sank a little closer to the earth of my position in response to the pull of that gravity which instills it.

This is a brief book and it would be unseemly for it to have other than a brief preface. But writing a book is a most intimate experience and inevitably it involves one's friends. Mrs. Nancy Andrews of the library of the San Diego Fine Arts Museum provided me with working space from which I might look out on some of the splendid pieces in the museum's sculpture garden. The writing begun in San Diego was continued aboard that most amiable and gracious of all conceivable inventions of human travel, the *France*. I wish especially to thank M. Jean Cloarec who during the days of several voyages placed my chair judiciously, so that I might enjoy not only fresh air but solitude as well. The library of the University of Arizona, particularly in the person of Mrs. Mary McWhorter, has also been most helpful, as indeed has my long-time friend and former colleague, Mrs. Elizabeth Shaw of the University of Arizona Press. During the period of revision I enjoyed the good hospitality of Mr. and Mrs. James Wahlman, and of Mr. John Bird and Mr. Robert Coons. Mr. and Mrs. Charles Benton, toward whom my affection and gratitude are great, have with generous warmth given both their friendship and hospitality. They particularly, together with Mr. Eric Frey, and Professor and Mrs. Jack Berry, proved most steadfast during a difficult period when my life was most in flux. Professors Earl W. Count, Charles Keil, and Dan Ben Amos have read and helpfully commented upon an earlier version of this work. I am especially indebted to them. Mr. William J. McClung of the University of California Press, acting in the best tradition of the creative editor, has gently led me to a significant revision of the two final chapters of the book. It is my pleasure here, in the book he has helped to create, to record my gratitude.

Introduction

Humanistic anthropology, like any other humanistic study, is concerned with the varieties, the qualities, and through these the nature and the value of human experience. It is not dedicated to the simple description of institutions, nor to reductions, nor to models. Quantification is not significant in humanistic anthropology, unless it is bent toward the end of illuminating the lived process of being human. This is not to say that the humanistic anthropologist is without interest in structures, for insofar as he is a humanist he shares a tradition of studying the patterns of being human that long antedate the structural interests of the social anthropologist. But the structures with which he is concerned are those of human experience. Sadly, humanists do not always keep their priorities clearly in mind and so sometimes make their means their end. They become enamored with the composition of a painting, or with the trajectory of an empire, or with the imagery of a poet—all these for their own sakes rather than for man's. They are "humanists" by name only. Mere subject matter distinguishes them from social scientists. They do not perceive that in these phenomena all that is significant is the presence of *man being*.

Humanistic anthropology is this genuine, human concern projected into the multi-cultured field embraced by anthropology conventionally defined. Despite the presence of *anthropology* in the phrase, humanistic anthropology shares neither the methods nor the objectives of regular anthropology. At its simplest, anthropology is to be seen as the study of man's institutions, "behavior," and a limited number of rubrics (technology, politics, and so forth) that are held to be wholly adequate to comprehending the rich fabric of human culture. Traditional anthropology is chiefly dedicated to the objectives of testing often small hypotheses of structure or process which are culture- (or even village-) specific; more rarely it is devoted to the perception of general uniformities behind the welter of data from various cultures. Humanistic anthropology, on the other hand, is the study of the condition and the experience of being a human being. It is dedicated to the understanding and the appreciation of man. It has a grid to be sure, which it places on human activity, for it is inevitable that out of the rich diversity and full dimension of human experience selection should occur. But the structures of this grid are at their best subtler than those of traditional anthropology, less determined by a narrow, mechanistic, reductivistic, and often trivial view of man. This book is an effort in humanistic anthropology, but its scope and purpose are modest, for humanistic anthropology is quite new and steps that will appear undramatic to the casual observer must be taken first.

Humanistic anthropology recognizes the essentially obscure, nonverbal, aconceptual nature of much of human experience and so seeks "evidence" different from that of traditional anthropology. The social anthropologist searches for hard data, rejecting the presumably soft evidence the humanistic anthropologist finds critical. The difference between hard and soft is the difference between seeing evidence as a neat behavioristic reduction of human being into tidy and quantifiable categories (hard) and in contrast seeing it as a complexity of imponderables and ambiguities. The humanistic anthropologist attempts to perceive in these ambiguities what regularities he can. He is interested in an array of pictures of man's inner reality—impressionistic, soft-edged, fuzzy, or sharp—knowing them all to be of some value and to constitute portions of the subtle wholeness of the lived world.

But all anthropologists share the view that human activity is patterned and that these patterns coalesce to constitute cultures. In this book I am interested in that inner and often enormously obscure principle, or dynamic factor, that determines the shapes and the dynamics of that coalescence.

For those who are interested in such classification, perhaps I ought to observe that humanistic anthropology seems to me less a science than an art. This means that multiple perspectives are not only inevitable but desirable, which in turn means that there are neither right nor wrong answers. There are only observations and postulations—analyses and constructs either plausible or implausible, liberating or restricting, seminal or barren, ones that illumine or ones that obfuscate. The value of a study in humanistic anthropology depends upon the creativity of the worker, upon his ability to perceive new relationships among well-known data. The people about whose cultures such observations are written—such configurations descried—may or may not be aware of them. But this is not relevant. It is the task of the humanistic anthropologist to make meaningful constructions that extend our knowledge of the range of the possibilities of living human life. It is, in a sense, creative or imaginative anthropology that the humanistic anthropologist practices.

One is a humanistic anthropologist for the simple reason that he enjoys a passionate concern to perceive something of the outlines of that nearly inscrutable condition of being human. I write "nearly inscrutable" because human being is so massive and recondite, and because the observer is after all part of what he observes, that the perceiving of it is fraught with problems. The humanistic anthropologist wishes to know the range of human being, and within that range what is genuine diversity and what is but a situational variant. Where is that substratum at which all peoples, despite their local cultural diversities, are similar? And *what* is that substratum? What is the nature of culture? Why is it patterned? We know well enough *how* it is patterned, but as to its cause we know very little indeed. Is there a root determination to the shape and the processes of a culture? Are there multiple causes? Or is this a false question? And is culture begun and does it move as a system, a historical phenomenon whose regularities have evolved in the battle against existential entropy?

These are the kinds of questions that engage the humanistic anthropologist. In a word he wishes to gain prise upon one face of that living and human phenomenon called culture. This is what makes him an anthropologist. In this particular work, I shall pursue this objective by exploring areas of human experience to which most anthropologists have paid scant attention. Accordingly, there are no pat anthropological procedures appropriate to this study.

Man is both the focus and the raison d'être of humanistic anthropology. It is an irony that this should be the respect in which humanistic is to be distinguished from social anthropology. But it follows from this, although perhaps not as inalienably as one might at first suppose, that the humanistic anthropologist, in contrast with the social anthropologist, neither thinks he is "value-free" nor regards this estate as either possible or desirable.

The humanistic anthropologist yearns for value, to paraphrase St. Thomas, as matter yearns for form. He flees to it for the simple reason that value is the medium within which he exists as a man. As it is difficult for man adequately to observe and to assess that universe of value within which he exists, because it is the inescapable ground of his being, so is it also impossible for him to be value-free. It is wistful even to regard it as desirable that he should be so. The humanistic anthropologist is therefore involved in value—conscientiously so, and at best judiciously as well. It is the *quality* of situation, belief, and experience with which he is concerned.

The primary tenet of the humanistic anthropologist is that what the social anthropologist is wont to call "behavior" is in reality, when viewed from the perspective of the person who is "behaving," *experience*. Humanistic anthropology is thus an inner rather than an outer anthropology. But it rests on a paradox, for in fact all that can be known of the inner is what is outer. So the difference between the two anthropologists is a

difference between their perspectives on human action
and not wholly a difference in the kinds of human actions
with which one is concerned. In the long run these
differences in perspectives amount to major differences
between the fields. The social anthropologist looking at
human actions perceives not human experiences but
merely structures to which experience is irrelevant. In
religion he perceives the structure of the priesthood, the
liturgical calendar, the obligations of the communicants,
and the array of religious estates, their characteristics
and the conditions under which these occur. The humanistic anthropologist perceives all of these, too. But
this is not his objective. He prefers to regard these as
but the delineaments of a pattern whose significance
lies in human experience and is yet to be found. At the
very least his every word is addressed to the proposition
that it is the estate of human being with which he is
concerned.

The study of that spectrum of human experience
called "art" and which I name the universe of the
affecting presence is a prime case in point. The social
anthropologist, because of his special preoccupations, is
precluded from apprehending the affecting presence as
it is and so when he takes it into account at all, which
is seldom enough, he does so in terms not only inadequate but indeed even irrelevant to it. The social anthropologist thus does not perceive the work of affecting
presence. Indeed he sees nothing of a culture that makes
it what it is—a lived and living plexus of people both
palpably and impalpably *being*.

Of course the social anthropologist does not wish to
study this seething, lived universe. But nonetheless this
world of living phenomenality is there to be studied and

there are those among us not only those who wish to study it rather than anything else, but who also believe that it is profoundly important to do so if we are to come closer to living man. And so the humanistic anthropologist makes his beginning where culture is presented to him, persuaded both that culture is experience and that it reveals itself in its own terms. Thus the humanistic anthropologist turns his attention to sculptures themselves, to music as music, to rite as enactment, to culture itself as a presentation of its own imperatives which, rather as chromosomes inform every bodily cell, instill each conceivable cultural action with the preconditions of its own possibility.

Since humanistic anthropology is an art rather than a science (by which I mean that it is dedicated to the illumination of experience and not to the definition of some item of "reverifiable knowledge") alternative propositions are possible for any given culture. The ultimate legitimation of any proposition is to be found in the satisfaction it provides as an explication and an illumination of culture and in the range of cultural phenomena it will accommodate. The principle of elegance prevails. That proposition which most easily and most simply accounts for the broadest range of experience will provide the deepest satisfaction and hence will also enjoy the widest validity. Such propositions can be developed either by those who are of or those who are alien to the culture; by those aliens who work solely with the presented phenomena as well as by those who also wish to take into account the testimonies of informants. It makes no difference. Each can achieve the formulation of a proposition equally eligible for scrutiny.

In directing his attentions to the experienced phenomena of a culture, the humanistic anthropologist is taking a significant and a revolutionary step. The way is therefore not always clear and we may be disappointed with the early results. I recall an interested student who expressed such disappointment. She had expected my work to reveal *more*—something wholly new and transforming. I share that regret. But I have confidence that as humanistic anthropology grows precisely such results will be forthcoming. So far, in my own work, I have been able only to propose the most elementary spatiotemporal preconditions for experience in the cultures of but two peoples. And yet, as simple and as elementary as these propositions may appear to be, they represent an advance in our understanding of man, for previously we had known nothing at all of such preconditions. Indeed we had only half suspected their existence on those rare occasions when we considered the "integration" of the arts.

In my view we have not searched deeply enough either to see the most basic principles at work or to perceive their significance, which is that culture is of a sameness because it derives from a common proto- or *ur-*, or paleo-proposition, that is aconceptual and is omnipresently existential. It is to the perception and the delineation of this progenerative imperative in the universe of experience—lying determinedly, if enigmatically, at the root of all the phenomena of culture, giving to them an identity and an order—that humanistic anthropology is dedicated. It is also to such a perception that this book is devoted. I have chosen to enter into a consideration of this progenerative force through a further reckoning with the affecting presence, which is our point of entry.

PART ONE

The Affecting Presence
and Consciousness

1

Anthropology, Aesthetics, and the Affecting Presence

Aesthetics for the anthropologist is best defined as the *theory or study of form incarnating feeling.* Perhaps we ought to say "incarnating affect" since *feeling* might be construed in too restricted a sense, notably in the romantic sense of a specific emotion—of joy, sadness, or some such—about a specific situation or thing. Indeed a work may be created not to incarnate a feeling at all, but rather an unaccountable and basic fact of one's awareness, about which one feels significantly. Thus, as we shall see, it is possible to incarnate in the affecting presence not only "beauty," which we may presume to be the result of a special relationship between the sensuous and the conceptual features of a work, a particular individualistic emotion, but also any of the infinite points on a spectrum of other realities, even including the very primal stuff of the universe as it is presumed by a particular people to be.

In such cases, those specific properties of the affecting presence we in European cultures most readily respond to will not be as important to witnesses co-cultural with a work of art as they are to those to whom the immediacy of the affecting presence is subjugated to a philosophy of *art*, which is a manifestation of a highly self-conscious perfectionism that brings every feature of a work into explicit and notable control often for the simple sake of such control. Thus virtuosity comes to be of significance. Instead, in such cultures as contrast with this situation *essential, basic, general* formal conditions tend to be defined for works, and these works tend to exist as instances of classes, as for example among the Yoruba any given pair of *ibeji* is to be regarded as a subspecies of the class of twin figures, which is to be seen in large measure as a class of functions—namely those of incarnating the essence of the twin, and of being efficacious with respect to the well-being of the twin.

But beyond this expectation of class conformity, not too much more may be required, for example with respect to the factor of virtuosity—at least not to the extent one might anticipate, since two works of unequal excellence but of the same class may in any given appropriate situation be judged to be equally efficacious. This is the case, for example, among the Ekiti Yoruba where an aged Epa mask may be retired to be replaced by another that to the European may seem less good. This class-effective concept, however, together with the beauty concept does not exhaust the possibilities. For example the class concept of the affecting presence may prevail, as in Java, and yet the "art" value may also obtain simultaneously. Two wooden puppets depicting Ardjuna, either of which may satisfactorily enact the role, are discriminated one from the other and evaluated in terms of the virtuosity of their conformation and their execution.

It is clear therefore that there is no *single* aesthetic prescript for all cultures. There is the possibility of formulating many aesthetics, each devoted to describing or explaining in particular cultures *how it is* that works embody affect. It is for this reason that we cannot go further and, for instance, make categorical statements such as that which asserts unequivocally that the affecting work is a symbol; for even if this were true of our own culture, as I believe it is *not*, it would clearly be untrue of a culture in which the chief value of an affecting presence is that *it directly bears* power.

It is factually true that the affecting presence is not in its distinctive and definitive sense a symbol, though it may, and indeed often does, also bear symbolic attributes. Rather it directly presents affect. It is only in this sense, namely that form does incarnate affect, that it may be said that there is a universal aesthetic. Over and above this universal fact are to be found those variations which ultimately proliferate into a particular system of aesthetics. These inescapable conditions define the basic epistemological ground upon which the student of human being must work. It is to a consideration of this situation of universal and variable—to an examination of how it is that the affecting presence is in every culture directly presentational, incarnating what is culturally important, and yet how at the same time it has significant variability from culture to culture—that this book is dedicated.

An adequate anthropological study of aesthetics, then, must take its point of departure in the acceptance of this diversity, and it must account for it. It must illuminate specific aesthetic systems, and in so doing must show in detail how the cultural individuality of affecting works in all forms is accounted for; it must show the specific features of shape and dynamics which are the minimal conditions of affecting acceptance, and must offer, at least as hypothesis, the cultural principle that ordains that these be so.

To construct such a study of aesthetics in current anthropology is difficult: the nature of the affecting presence is not understood; an inhospitable mis-en-scène prevails in the study of culture; unsuspected ethnocentrisms obscure our perceptions. In short, anthropology is generally executed in a fashion that precludes the discovery of the aesthetic system. We must permit the anthropologist to come to grips with affecting phenomena in terms of the self-proclaimed and self-compelling dictates of the nature of the works with which he is concerned.

An adequate theory of the affecting presence depends upon an adequate theory of culture, which in turn depends upon an adequate theory of man, and this is the crux of the problem. Theories of culture are not going to be ameliorated as long as the prevalent view of man is as a learning animal.

One sometimes suspects that the tactics, solicitations, analyses, classifications, and subsequent structurings of the anthropologist divide the wholeness of an alien lived-world into structures more familiar perhaps to the anthropologist than to the people who live the culture he writes about. This is in no instance more true than it is in the area of aesthetics, where it seems gratuitously to be presumed, as a starting point, that the explicit category of *the aesthetic* itself is universal. This is to say it is presumed that all people speculate specifically upon such matters. More often than not, it appears to be the case that an ethnocentric *crypto-aesthetics* of the anthropologist links the affecting presence, as a universal cultural phenomenon, with the notion of the "beautiful," a notion so obscure in our own culture that I am left breathless at the confidence with which an outsider—which is to say an European—will undertake such inquiry in a foreign culture. In any case, it is tacitly presumed that the category of "the beautiful" is universal, and that the difficulty in ascertaining its presence in its cultural bed lies in the fact that the particular object is subjected to little philosophical inquiry among many of the people one studies, or else that "beauty" is a topic upon which the informants are—for whatever reason of secrecy, obtuseness, or obstinacy—vague. That in the first respect there is not always an explicitly developed aesthetic, we ought to be persuaded by the numerous failures of those who have set out to find such systems. That the expectation of finding an aesthetic (*practiced*, as opposed to *formulated*) of *beauty* is equally ethnocentric, I shall demonstrate subsequently.

The shortcomings of traditional anthropology with respect to the appropriate perception of the affecting presence derive also from the fact that traditional anthropology is *social* anthropology and the social dimension of the affecting presence is clearly not its distinctive and essential feature. Indeed, by concentrating upon the *social*, as he usually understands it, the anthropologist is placed in the paradoxical and deprived position of missing in the affecting presence that which is in the final analysis profoundly, ever so subtly, and indeed—in the *root* sense of the word—radically social. For in eloquent but traditionally implicit ways, the affecting presence *presents* those profound conditions which make social existence possible.

The social anthropologist changes terms—from those

presented by the phenomenon to designations of quantity, structure, or other mensurations that are extrapolations from and not essential properties of the work. Most often what is produced does not portray lived structures and functions. So it is that the social scientist, confronting the affecting presence, studies what the phenomenon significantly *is not* rather than what it significantly *is*. The term "humanistic anthropology" names the stratagem by means of which I hope to define objectives and to establish procedures in terms of which man is to be seen in his *human* diversity—as well as his commonality—to be studied and appreciated in that experiential reality that differentiates him from all other classes of sentient life. Before a humanistic anthropology can be achieved, the model of man as social animal must yield before the model of man as rich, subtle, spiritual, rational—whole, conscious, and experiencing. This is the view underlying all the statements concerning the affecting presence made in this book.

It is the aim of a humanistic anthropology to turn our curiosity, our sense of insatiable wonder, our rich imagination away from the *hows* and the *how-manys* of culture to its *qualities*, for it is in culture's qualities and its textures that we find the rich, inextricable, and constitutive maze of experience wherein solely lies all that is human in culture. Through the experience-yielding attributes and the qualities of the *whats* of culture, we may reach the threshold of that perception wherein people, places, and things are seen as unique to the particular culture. Through a qualitative confrontation are dry data and sterile networks transmuted into the lusty metabolism of experience of which both the people who live the culture and the humanistic anthropologist who seeks it are alike enamored. The aim of humanistic anthropology, in a word, is the discovery of the lived cultural world, or the culturality of the lived world.

It is possible that this anthropology of experience, like other forms of the contemplation of the qualities of human cultures, might lead merely to inarticulate appreciation—or, as in the case of some literary criticism, to articulate unappreciation. Yet inarticulate appreciation is a reaction more nearly *in kind* with that phenomenon which excites our wonder than is its translation into those vitiated extrapolations which are neither the object of contemplation nor even a reasonable approximation of it. Humanistic anthropology, thus, can be described as a spectrum of attentions, from abject and nonverbal apprehension to a less mystical though perhaps no less ecstatic attempt to perceive the cultural *whats* more reliably in somewhat more appropriately analytical terms. Because it is an *anthropology* with which we are concerned, this attempted perception is to be accomplished in terms dictated by the culture whose works we confront—or rather, whose works confront us, insisting ever so eloquently, ever so intransigently, upon the validity and the propriety of their own existence in their own terms.

Such an objective, however, poses serious questions and subtle puzzles. It also requires that we re-examine the purposes for which we pursue anthropological inquiry. The first question is not a new one—indeed it is as ancient, in all probability, as the recognition of the fact that while *self-other* exists on a continuum, there is a point beyond which each man is absolutely and abjectly

isolable from all others, each in the unique particularity
of his unknowable difference. The same differentiation
that obtains among men of one culture, even between
brothers, obtains even more markedly among men of
different cultures. There is that ultimate point at which
two cultures also are finally and utterly isolated one
from the other, each immured in those definitive and
constitutive differences which, like the insignificant spatial difference between the location of the two eye-sock-
ets of a skull in Poe's *The Gold Bug*, carried through
the measurement of time, become ever more significant
the farther one moves from the base point.

Certain questions arise if we pause long enough to
think of our own procedures against the background
of this awareness. Are the intellectual structures with
which we encounter another culture sufficiently subtle
to permit one to perceive the difference between himself,
the man of the querying culture, and the man of the
responding culture? Or are they, rather, unsuspectedly
ethnocentric and thus invalidated by a hopeless myopia
which permits only the most limited understanding,
precluding the fullest possible comprehension of and
enrichment from the alien culture with which one is
confronted? If our objective is the simple accretion of
knowledge in our own terms and forms, then traditional
methods of anthropological inquiry serve us well. If,
however, the end of one's anthropology is not data but
understanding, if its end is not the *science of man* but
the art of man, or the art of being human, then such
methods are both inadequate and inapposite.

I am not aware that a culture has ever been described
as a *pattern-in-experience*, which seems strange because
if culture is anything it is pattern and meaning, signifi-

cance, consequence, feeling, experience: *consciousness*, in a word; and its locus must be in the breast and head and skin of each of those individual persons who by history and consent constitute it. So it follows that we have had views of the *whats* of culture as artifacts, as functions, as symbols, as communications—but not as foci of experience, of consciousness. The artifactual view of the *what* is nullified by the reductive fallacy; the functional view by the mechanistic fallacy; and the symbolic and communicational views, though both nearer the mark, by substitutive and translational fallacies—each of them removing what is studied from the definitive matrix of its experience.

These are all to be seen in the anthropological approaches to the study of the affecting presence in culture. The affecting presence is not to be approached merely as an object, nor simply as a function, nor only as a symbol or a communication. These considerations illuminate facets of the affecting presence, as indeed they illuminate facets of a person; but not all together, and certainly not singly, do they account for that profound and profoundly misperceived work which is the affecting presence. The affecting presence is at least a direct presentation of the feelingful dimension of experience. It proceeds at its root not through mediation, as a symbol does—though it may do this as well—but through what we may only call *immediation*. The affecting presence is directly and presently what it is, and precisely *is* in those physical-significant terms in which it is presented for our witnessing. My use of this term "witnessing" rather than "viewing" or "seeing" or "hearing" or "perceiving" is intended to suggest not only that the confrontation between man and work is an *act* but also

that it is an act of consequence to which the role of
witness is of critical importance.

What we behold in the affecting presence is less of
the world of object than a phenomenon of the personal
world of man—not a utensil but an act ever in the process
of enacting itself—an instance of incarnated experience,
and the *sole* instance of a man's and a culture's interiority available to the outsider. So it is that the
affecting work is not a member of a class of things apart
from the life of the culture, negligible to the anthropologist, but a metaphoric celebration of the dynamic
and the constitution of the world. The study of the
affecting presence is the study of man in those terms
which finally are his definitive ones, that is to say those
that comprise the elements of the process of living-as-a-
man. His presented experience in the affecting presence
brings us his living forms, *the living forms of his consciousness.*

The affecting forms are a system and are special,
unique presentations of a culture. Though affecting
works may have ascribed, referential functions which
may serve to make symbols or signs of some of them,
nonetheless what they are in and of themselves are
presentations of being. Indeed insofar as a particular
work embodies the cultural form—that least common
denominator of particularity which uniquely establishes
one culture—it is a presentation of the basic and irreducible being of the culture. Great works, it goes without
contest, greatly incarnate these vitalities.

As it is difficult, given his present postulates, for the
traditional anthropologist to apprehend the real constitution of the affecting presence, so apparently it is for

the traditional aesthetician. Susanne Langer provides a case in point.

Upon first consideration, the reader may perceive only a few fundamentally important distinctions between Susanne K. Langer's *non-discursive symbol* and my *affecting presence*. Both are concerned with the work's presentation. Yet there are more profound differences. The affecting presence, in contrast to the non-discursive symbol, stresses the self-sufficiency of the work, such that once created it stands whole and wholly independent of either creator or witness; it stresses the work's persistence; it stresses its life in metaphor, its viability, its metabolism; it stresses its *personality*. The affecting presence is thus ontologically different from the non-discursive symbol.

Langer's view of the work of art as a symbol is developed in *Philosophy in a New Key*[1] and re-affirmed in both *Feeling and Form*[2] and *Problems in Art*.[3] The work of art, she says, is a symbol which symbolizes not the phenomena of the rational order but rather those of the universe of feeling. These phenomena, we are given to understand, have "logical" structures which are somehow simulated by the work of art.[4] Langer seems not to face the question of the respect in which the notion of a "logical" structure of a feeling somehow reduces the universe of feeling to the rules of the universe

[1] Susanne K. Langer, *Philosophy in a New Key: A Study in the Symbolism of Reason, Rite and Art* (Cambridge: Harvard University Press, 3rd ed., 1957).

[2] Susanne K. Langer, *Feeling and Form* (New York: Charles Scribner's Sons, paper, 1953).

[3] Susanne K. Langer, *Problems of Art* (New York: Charles Scribner's Sons, paper, 1957).

[4] Langer, *Feeling and Form*, p. 34.

of reason. In any case, by denying the possibility of the work of art's *actual presentation*, which she accomplishes by turning it into a symbol, she builds what would appear to be a self-contradictory argument. On the one hand she must assert that the work of art is not an actual feeling, and on the other hand she is forced to conceive that it is a symbol which in fact is not a symbol because it has no referent but rather incorporates the "logical" structure of what would ordinarily be its referent. She attempts to circumvent this predicament by speaking of the *presentational symbol*, but the question of whether the "symbol" is in fact "presentational" is not satisfactorily resolved since what it is presumably presentational of, namely the feeling's "logical" structures, has not satisfactorily been described, let alone proven to exist.

To Langer the work of art thus becomes an "illusion," a "semblance," a thing compounded of lies, or what she calls "virtual properties"—colors which are not the veritable colors of what is presented, sounds which are not its veritable sounds, and volumes which are not the veritable volumes of the feeling or the object or the experience with respect to which the work (as she would have it) stands in the relationship of semblance. Thus does Langer make of a silk purse a sow's ear! She achieves this reverse magic by virtue of too great a reliance on rationalism, on the ultimate legitimacy of reason and of reason's model. With respect to the domain of art, then, she is a disciplinary ethnocentric. She presents no persuasive evidence to support her actions in forcing the phenomena of feeling to conform to the models of the reason—and so does not perceive that this different universe of feeling in form may also have its unique forms and laws. Thus it is that, in my view, she misapprehends the ontological status of the work of art.

The aesthetic of energy for example—as we shall see it among the Yoruba—together with the nonsymbolic, immediately presentational, ontologically independent nature of the affecting presence refutes further details of Langer's theory, namely those pertaining to how we apprehend a work. If one believes the work is a symbol, he is going to develop a theory of apprehension which is consistent, involving proxies, models, and mediation—all designed to intervene between the observer and the observed. So it is that Langer maintains "that what art expresses in *not* actual feeling, but ideas of feeling," and yet she asserts a sentence or two later in the same paragraph that "It is not sensuously pleasing and *also* symbolic; the sensuous quality is in the service of its vital import."[5] Thus we have *ideas* and *logical structures* conveyed by symbols which are but illusions, but whose sensuous qualities actually somehow bear the "import," which is the significance of the work. This seems to me at best a paradox, but one which results not from the order of things but rather from the inadequate description of a phenomenon not fully or appropriately apprehended.

If I disagreed with Langer merely on the basis of my belief that a symbol has no necessary physical conformity to what it conveys, and that this obviously exempts the work of art from being considered as a symbol, while she maintains that there is that kind of symbol that is necessarily characterized by such conformity, then the issue would be but one involving

[5] Ibid., p. 59.

different definitions. But I have a very different case
to make. The point which *The Affecting Presence*[6]
develops is that the work is constituted, in a primordial
and intransigent fashion, of basic cultural, psychic conditions—not symbols of those conditions but specific
enactments—presentations—of those very conditions.
Thus it is clear that in its elementary spatio-temporal
existence the affecting presence is not a "semblance"
but an actuality. In these basic space-time dimensions
then it follows that the affecting presence is a thing
in its own terms, and in cultural terms it *presents* rather
than *represents*. Langer fails to see this because she does
not view the affecting presence at the level of culture
and so naturally cannot perceive the most apparent,
general constitutive dimensions of the affecting presence
which are at this level revealed.

Thus it is that the points Mrs. Langer does not take
into account, at any level or in any respect, are two,
and these are the *sine qua non* of the consideration of
any human act, that is to say, first, the fundamental
importance of the testimony of cultural variables, and,
second, the ground consideration of the nature of consciousness. Thus she commits herself to an arbitrary
view of the work of art. If all consciousness were directed
in apprehension—*intended*—in the same shapes which
is to say with the same structures and with identical
force, there would be no differences among either perceptions or the arts. For that matter there would probably be no differences among cultures. To put the case
another way, one can assert that the existence of dif-

[6] Robert Plant Armstrong, *The Affecting Presence: An Essay in
Humanistic Anthropology* (Urbana: University of Illinois Press, 1971).

ferences among perceptions and the arts entail differences in the processes of intending. Consciousness,
as phenomenologists tell us, exists only as intended
awareness through the agencies of the perceptions. Consciousness is directed *through* patterns culturally given,
for culture in the final analysis is precisely this structur-
ing, this array of ways through which we perceive
phenomena. Perception, and at the base of perception
consciousness, is shaped by and instilled with a culture-
energy of which we shall learn more subsequently. For
the moment let me say only that this is acquired
profoundly through the baby's first experiences in and
feelings about space and time.

Time and space are primordial emotional experiences,
and at the very beginning the baby human learns the
first principles of an informing intelligence whose structures and processes his culture has determined upon
and which is the root difference distinguishing his culture from another. Man, then, finding himself engulfed
in this emotionally charged and natively significant
ambient, and vitally but not consciously discovering
that his culture has so informed space-time, discovers
also that his culture, being coherent, has also with the
same impress informed the whole vast dimensions of
his feeling. History has thus evolved for that cultural
universe a principle in terms of which time and space
are purposefully and systematically exploited so as to
enact that informing intelligence that I have called the
cultural metaphoric base.[7] Upon this are erected certain
schemata that analyze and create the world by means
which, despite primary differences among the physical

[7] Ibid.

bases of the various arts, they are yet *similetically* equivalent one to another.

So it is that man employs these feeling-charged, spatio-temporal determinants of his existence, which present his world to him, *to present* to his world certain of his experiences and feelings and feeling-charged beliefs about his world which are not even to be approached by means of the symbols of ordinary discourse which can often name but can never create them. Thanks to his culture, he learns to do this through the imposition of certain kinds of restraints, certain schemata, upon this vast ambient of space and time; he learns to manage emotionality and value by means of the affecting presence. To appease his rationality, he learns other kinds of control—language, mensuration, and symbolic manipulation—by means of which he produces discourse and science.

Those schemata that order space and time into this special category of experience (emotion and value) are the schemata of the affecting presence. They undergird, indeed they constitute the essential parameters of affect. They are subtle and difficult to perceive, largely perhaps because works have specific content which is difficult to avoid and which therefore stands in the way of the apperception of the general, the cultural.

This is not the sole testimony of ethnoaesthetics against the Langerian view, however. Let us look to the question of what precisely is incarnated in a non-Western affecting presence. It is in general a characteristic of the African affecting presence that it possesses power. A mask, a drum, an ancestor figure is "fed" life or goods in sacrifice, and it endures not as a symbol of power but as power itself which can—for example in the case of some masks—strike dead the unwary noninitiate who, in violation of the laws governing the mask, might witness it.

This idea that African sculpture is affiliated with power has so long been familiar that it is difficult and pointless to try to recall where or from whom one first heard it. In any case, I here propose to accept as a hypothesis the idea that power—or force, or vitality, or energy, or dynamics—is in fact *at least one* of the informing principles of the Yoruba schema, and thus, lying deep in the region of the cultural metaphoric base, is a wellspring of the Yoruba affecting universe. In making this assumption, I shall have as my purpose to discover whether, to what extent, and in what fashion this hypothesis will order and accommodate in good and meaningful sense the significant features of the Yoruba affecting presence.

To begin with, I shall defer to the view of William Fagg, who asserts a relationship between dynamics and Yoruba affecting works, even though I think he fails to perceive the significance of this relationship. Indeed, he even questions whether this liaison is of any importance, asserting that the conception of dynamism "by itself ... might be of academic rather than practical importance in the study of tribal culture and art." On the contrary I believe an informing principle, granting the necessary immediacy between feeling and form in the affecting presence and granting the role of the informing principle in setting the mode of that metaphor which establishes such immediacy, must ever and wholly inform the work. Fagg writes,

> Of all the thousands of pre-industrial tribal philosophies in the world, it is unlikely that any two will ever be found identical; yet in this one funda-

mental respect they would seem to be all alike, that
their ontology is based on some form of dynamism,
the belief in immanent energy, in the primacy of
energy over matter in all things. That is to say that
whereas civilizations see the material world as consisting of static matter which can move or be moved
in response to appropriate stimuli, tribal cultures
tend to conceive things as four-dimensional objects
in which the fourth or time dimension is dominant
and in which matter is only the vehicle, or the
outward and visible expression, of energy or life
force. Thus it is energy and not matter, dynamic
and not static being, which is the true nature of
things . . . . By itself it might be of academic rather
than practical importance in the study of tribal
culture and art, but its corollary—that this force
or energy is open to influence by man through ritual
means—is the very basis of all tribal belief and
observance.[8]

Thus the physical world exists only with respect to
an infinite source of energy which its objects utilize in
order to enact their various processes. So we shall assume
that for the Yoruba the space-time ambient is premised
on a pervasiveness of primal energy, and that the initial
emotionality in which time and space are learned is an
emotionality culturally defined as appropriate to coping
with the cosmic energy, whether generalized or focused
in some event or in affecting presence. The young
Yoruba, we shall assume, soon learns—or *did* in those
days of the fullness of Yoruba traditional belief—that
all that *is* is characterized by energy: the creator god,
the lesser gods, the ancestors, man, the affecting pres-

[8] William Fagg, *Nigerian Images* (London: Lund Humphries, 1963),
pp. 122-123.

ence, and animals, plants, places, and things. Immanent to each object and animal in the world is energy, and the object or the person is merely the discernable *dimension* of that energy. This energy is both *constant* in the universe (since existence continues and does not appear to be possible without this constant energy) and *prime*, which is to say that the only degree to which it can inform an object or an animal is ever in accordance with the fullness of its force *as allotted* to the species of animal or category of event or object. There can be no fractional possession of this energy—not at least if the person or object is to endure.

Constancy and primeness, we shall assume, then, are the aspects of energy; and these aspects subsequently are created in the affecting presence. We must, if we are to approach some comprehension of the significance the affecting presence might have in traditional Yoruba society (as indeed in many another), realize that *it* (the affecting presence) *is the only effective and effectuating entity that it lies within the power of man to create in order to gain prise upon this fundamental cosmological principle of energy which informs him as well as his stars.*

We may assume that energy is constant on the basis that new entities enacting it are ever coming into being, as former entities dissipate. And so there is a necessary appositional complementarity between matter and energy which is the principle that defines the nature of the Yoruba metaphoric process, rendering the work into power—always immanent, sometimes weak, sometimes rampant. Form needs energy to function, while energy needs form to have locus and efficacy. This complementarity is to be seen, for example, in the existence

among the Yoruba of a belief in ancestorism—in terms
of which upon the death of the individual his personalized energy is returned to the infinite, though with its
individuality yet ineradicably stamped on it—and in
reincarnation, in terms of which that force is returned
to living, human form. Both of these beliefs involve the
idea of the permanence of personalized energy and the
transitoriness of form. Man dies to become ancestor to
become once again reincarnated in human form. The
primeness of energy is to be read in this very cycle of
growth, decay, rebirth. The body needs energy to survive,
and it holds its quota of energy only so long as it is
capable of doing so, for power is abrasive; it wears its
vessel away; when the vessel is no longer sufficient to
its energy it dies, the energy itself to seek out new and
more adequate forms.

The access of the world's multitudinous items to this
universal energy is variable, depending not only upon
the placement of a given item in the hierarchy of things
but also upon its own particular condition of physical
and spiritual well-being. Further, energy at prime can
maximally infuse only things and beings in their prime;
for only such entities are equal to their appropriate and
full measure of power. That people may have their
energy diminished is attested to by the facts that they
fall victims to bad luck, that they grow ill, weaken, and
die. The science of healing is premised upon the notion
that the ailing individual can be returned to oneness
with prime energy. Similarly the well-being of the state
is based upon the premise that civil well-being is dependent upon the most optimal relation of the political
structure to the prime universal energy.

So it is that things age and their relationship with

energy becomes attenuated. In some cases, however, prime energy can be restored, and so we see that energy is manipulable, whether by the gods or by man, through special means of energy exchange (rite and sacrifice) which are exercised solely to bring about the optimal state of energy equilibrium. Energy, further, is equally the requisite of both gods and men. Thus while men through sacrifice manipulate and exercise in behalf of their own power, the gods themselves also similarly *require* sacrifices. It was in recognition of this need that Eshu, the Yoruba messenger and trickster god, was assigned the task of delivering offered sacrifices to Olorun, the supreme creator god. Energy is the economy of the soul and sacrifice is its coin; it is the means by which not only both men and gods are enriched but also, like them, the affecting presence. It too drinks in the released energy of the sacrificial victim or preparation, thus increasing itself by that allotted fullness of power.

According to this view, then, the universe of the affecting presence is not one of apartness and special nature, nor of irrelevance as we in the Western world have permitted our philosophers to make it appear to be. Rather the affecting work takes its place in the culturally defined order of things, as being of the same order of phenomena as all other works and objects in the world and as being metaphysically indistinguishable from them. Within the affecting presence lies energy, of which form is the visible dimension. The problem of the affecting presence is therefore, from this point of view, a problem in metaphysics, and so to assume the presence of an aesthetic of "beauty" is in error, and to imagine a conceptualized and discrete category of

speculation about the affecting universe as an order of
reality that is special and different from all others is
probably unwarranted: a tyranny of ethnocentrism, and
thus the reason why field workers fail to find the
autochthonous "aesthetic system" of the Yoruba.

If we are to seek the general outlines of a Yoruba
aesthetic we must witness the Yoruba affecting works
to ascertain in them what we can of the ontology of
energy and how it is that energy directly incarnates
through the processes of metaphor into those forms
which self-sufficiently and directly (in no wise like the
symbol), and purposefully and inalienably, present energy and generate that affect proper to the recognition
and experience of its presence.

Energy in the affecting work is of two sorts: substantive energy, which derives from the notion of the work's
content—as some of the energy of the Discus Thrower
derives from the fact that a man is about to throw a
discus—and metaphoric energy, which eventuates from
the activities of the various incarnative processes by
means of which the work comes into being and persists.
Since Yoruba works seldom convey substantive energy,
it follows that we shall be concerned here with the
energies of metaphor, by means of which base matter
is transmuted into important affect.

We may speak of two different kinds, or orders, of
metaphor in the affecting work—one *direct*, the other
substitutive. Direct metaphors of energy explicitly embody energy, within the system of convention established and accepted by the people. Substitutive metaphors are classes of metaphors, or are metaphoric
principles, and constitute the operative power which
governs the equation of direct metaphors of given sorts

across media and across forms. It is the substitutive metaphor with which I was concerned in *The Affecting Presence*. Here I shall be engaged with direct metaphor.

" ... images," Robert F. Thompson says, "show a concentrated expression of vitality tempered by balance and a sense of moral depth. The quality of commanding power ... forms an analogue to the notion of force and an ontology of being which has characterized much of the thinking of William Fagg about sub-Saharan creativity."[9] Thus does he seem to see the relationship between energy and art, in general terms, by means of a direct metaphor. I write "seems to" because while he speaks of an "ontology of being" and while he does suggest an equation between the power of the work and the power of the universe, yet he uses the word "analogue," which more invokes symbol than metaphor. In any case, this is a promising beginning. But we can perceive even more direct metaphors at work, directly constituting energy by virtue of generating it through several distinct processes.

We may consider first the factor of the primeness of energy in the affecting presence. Here we see that a sculpture—or for that matter a drum—is subject to the same fluctuations of energy as the earth or a king. All of them require sacrifices to maintain their powers. As long as affecting works are adequate to that energy which they command on behalf of man they are kept; when they are no longer adequate they are discarded. Often, though by no means always, the age of a work is evidence of its alienation from energy. When it is no

[9] Robert Farris Thompson, *Black Gods and Kings* (Los Angeles: University of California, Occasional Papers of the Museum and Laboratories of Ethnic Arts and Technology, 1971, Vol. II), p. 20/1.

longer young, it is in all probability no longer equal
to the high charges of prime energy characteristic of
items of its class. This fact is surely related to that
phenomenon Thompson calls "ephebism," the presentation in sculpture of human beings at the zenith of their
powers. Thus is a twin figure carved as at its maturity,
even though the actual twin be but a babe; and a votive
piece depicting a donor, who may very well in fact be
aged, enacts a figure (of the donor) in the prime of life.
Both sacrifice, therefore, and ephebism are to be seen
as presentations of the primeness of energy in sculpture;
they are actualizations of the primeness of the universal
energy.

Continuity and intension, to whose discussion much
of *The Affecting Presence* is devoted, also embody the
primeness of energy. Continuity presents this primeness
by virtue of asserting the ineluctable and omnipresent
prevailing of energy. Under the auspices of this understanding we may appreciate afresh the constitution of
temporal forms by a singular density of events and of
visual forms by a similar density of decorative details.
The so-called Yoruba baroque is thus to be seen as an
achievement of duration in primeness. Intension in
Yoruba works reinforces the primacy of continuity by
dramatizing it. But intension is also in its own right
a process in the creation of its own direct metaphor
of prime energy. There is an energy to mere intension,
as a wound spring, being intensive, is taut and potent
with created though conserved energy. Withal the spring
is composed and wholly present, as a Yoruba affecting
work is composed and wholly present.

But if we are to pursue our hypothesis of an aesthetic
of energy, there are three other processes to be seen,

processes which are, however, doubtless subsequent to intension and continuity, the basal metaphors of experienced space and time. These are the processes of complementarity, repetition and hyperbole. Like intension and continuity, these processes are, once created, constantly operative in the work—constantly kinetic, constantly eventuating states of affecting affairs. These processes do not enact continuity and intension; they are not of spatio-temporal *shape*,[10] but of spatio-temporal process, and they enact within the work both an interior and a surface which are vital with energy-in-process.

Yoruba works of sculpture are powerfully composed networks of various systems of energy-achieving and energy-achieved tensions. By means of complementarity, which is to be seen as the fulfilling relationship among points on a continuum in order that the continuum itself might be achieved, tension comes to exist as a function of the very process of achieving completeness. It exists between the work fulfilling and the work fulfilled, between creating energy and conserving it, between being prime and being transient, between being energy and being form, all of which are successive phases in being. This is complementarity with respect to the whole of prime energy, of which the portion of the work itself is but a visible and vital iota. But there is complementarity *within* the work as well—among its parts—deriving from a studied exploitation of the principle of two-ness. This internal two-ness, next after intensionality and continuity, seems to be the root cause of the over-riding dynamic of Yoruba affecting presentations. This principle defines the system of points among

[10] Although continuity and intension are processes as well—processes which eventuate in shape.

which fancy operates, caroming from one possibility to
another in an eternal motion which contributes to the
energy of the work.

The chief agency of this internal complementarity
characterizing nearly every Yoruba work—indeed, nearly
as inevitably as intensive-continuity—is *balance* or *symmetry*, which is achieved by means of the identical
statement of comparable parts, the adjacency of apposite points along a continuum. Yoruba work stresses
not the *opposition* of opposites, as Western works do,
but rather the simple contiguity of complementary
points, the apposition of apposites. Balance is a rhetoric
of appositions which is ever in the process of proclaiming
itself. This we must take to be a metaphoric presentation
of an aspect of the nature of energy, saying of it that
under ideal circumstances it is in dynamic apposition
to the whole as indeed the work itself is apposite to
the order of the universe.

The energy process of this balance in Yoruba affecting
works is so essential that Thompson says of it, "In
Yorubaland . . . mature expression and lack of balance
are mutually exclusive."[11] Balance is a direct metaphor
of a further fact of the nature of energy—by as much
as the forms of the world are robbed of energy, by so
much must energy be restored to them; by as much
as earth is spent in its endless rounds of providing, by
so much must earth be renewed, through rain, through
prayer, through sacrifice.

This form of appositional balance may exist in the
particularly energetic form of *compression*, which obviously becomes itself an especially seminal metaphor
for energy. We perceive compression most basically

[11] Thompson, *Black Gods*, p. 17/3.

perhaps in the twofold nature of intensionality—as reinforcement of continuity as well as metaphor in its own right. Energy abounds when the witness's realization throughout the total process of his interaction with the affecting presence constantly ricochets from one significance to the other.

Robert Thompson, in *Black Gods and Kings*, first provided me with insight into the compressed metaphor of the Yoruba affecting work. Describing a thunder-god pedestal," upon which sacred stone celts are kept, Thompson writes:

> It is a masterpiece of visual word play. First the two conical masses of the stand recall the two celts from heaven which adorn the end of the axe of the deity. Secondly, there seems to be a certain degree of conscious overlapping with the hourglass shape of the bata drums for the thundergod. The careful balancing of two couples, male and female (plate 1), unites the two conical masses.[12]

This phenomenon, which he elsewhere in the same work refers to as "visual punning," one recognizes to be relatively common among Yoruba sculptures in the *ose Sango* (plates 2, 3, 4, 5) in which the double-headed axe motif is often confounded with a head-tie, or is wholly transfigured into a janus-head.

Just as he perceives the phenomenon of the compressed metaphor, without naming it, so does Thompson perceive that kind of affect about affecting works which we shall here call paradox, understanding by the term the juxtaposition not of real but rather of *only apparent* contrarieties—the mere adjacency of what might appear to be opposites, but what are in fact to be viewed rather

12 Ibid., p. 12/5.

as but points along a continuum. These points are made
adjacent by virtue of a collapsing process which elimi-
nates intervening points, thus abutting points which
normally are separated.

> The contrast between the calm of the mask and
> the great energy of the whirling, stamping, and
> turning dances which compose most festivals for
> Gelede might be compared to the binary oppositions
> within the praise literature of the goddess of the
> sea.[13]

The paradox of complementarity eventuates when
two or more apparently contradictory terms or conditions simultaneously exist in the same affecting work
or event *in relationship* one with the other. Paradox,
Molara Ogundipe tells us, " . . . pleases Yoruba very
much,"[14] and knowing this one therefore searches for
other instances of the process, to find his labor rewarded
in that relationship which the affecting work presents
between energy and one of its forms—which is to say
between the eternal and the transient. The resolution,
unexpected by those of us in the Western world, is that
the paradox in the final analysis falls apart: the energy
remains ever strong but gradually—as it were—oxidizes
the piece—and man himself—so that the form weakens
and deteriorates. Thus in the long run the entity itself
is no longer viable and is therefore disposed of. Here
we see not a process of opposition, but the strength of
process, the transitory fading before the onrush of the
overwhelming eternal.

There is a further fundamental paradox in instances

[13] Ibid., p. 14/5.

[14] Molara Ogundipe, "*The Palm-Wine Drinkard*—A Re-Assessment,"
Leadan, 1970, No. 28, p. 25.

of the Yoruba affecting presence as between the general and the specific. This derives from the fact that there is among the Yoruba a clear sense of genre—as in the genre of *ose Sango*—which of course is clearly socialized and therefore strong. Nonetheless there is much invention permitted within the demands of the genre as anyone can see if he but takes the trouble to examine the specimens of *ose Sango* here illustrated. This very inventiveness in the juxtaposition of the specific work to the socialized nature of the genre creates a tension which is a dynamic internal and not external to the work. But here we also come full circle, for this tension is also the tension of complementarity, since in its essence the individual work reflects the general, even as man himself, despite his individuality, is a recurring form—sometimes, as in reincarnation and in twinning, identically so.

Hyperbole is a far less subtle process of energy generation, producing energy in a most immediate way by the very forces of exaggeration, by the extravagance of invention. More importantly, it endows its work with energy by virtue of an act which in its relationship to energy fits into the rationale of the energy of sacrifice. This is to say that the energy of one entity or thing is transferred to another. So it is with the hyperbole. The energy of the excessive, of the monstrous, the outrageous invention of which the Yoruba are often so fond, is created within the work and endows it with its charge. Indeed it may be said of all the metaphors which conspire to create affecting works that they are all sacrifices, in this sense of the word, to the affecting work—ways of augmenting that work's share of prime energy. With the process of repetition the case is even

simpler. As repeated blows of a hammer release increas-
ingly more energy so that the nail in being driven ever
more deeply into the wood accrues ever more energy,
so it is with the repeated element in the affecting work.
Repetition yields the energy of accrual.

In short, then, it is not only the case that the continuity of energy is metaphorized in intensive-continuity;
that its primeness is metaphorized in ephebism and
sacrifice; but also that its dynamism—its condition of
ever being in process—which is the third essential element in its composition, is created in the work's ever-en-
acting internal metabolic principles of complementarity,
hyperbole, and repetition. So it is, finally, that we have
had the opportunity to perceive, if only in the smallest
way, the possibility of an aesthetic alternative to the
aesthetic of beauty; we may with all this receive a
suggestion of something of the possible field of affect.
It is no longer adequate, for either the philosopher or
for the anthropologist, to be aesthetically ethnocentric.

Being an actualization in energy of the primordial
experience of space and time, and being a presentation
of the spatio-temporal parameters of consciousness itself, the affecting presence exists. It is not "virtual" or
illusory—it *is*, and herein lies the singular challenge to
both social anthropologists and symbol-infatuated aestheticians. Both of these scholars must come face to
face with the fact that the affecting presence is a direct
presentation of human *being*, and they must seize the
opportunity to approach this amazing phenomenon in
its own terms if their common objective of understanding man is to be realized.

Of course it is only surprising that Mrs. Langer should
not have avoided these pitfalls. She is not, after all, an
anthropologist. It is inexcusable that the thinking of

anthropologists should similarly have suffered from
having failed to take into consideration both the nature
of culture and the nature of man. So it is that the
anthropologist can be accused of having been inexplica-
bly naive in his consideration of the affecting presence,
abandoning himself to easy ethnocentric cliches. That
this should be the case reflects the lack of importance
accorded the affecting works of culture, a reflection of
the prevailing model-dictated reductions and epistemo-
logically, phenomenologically, and existentially inadequate extrapolations, truncations, and warpings of what
remains of behaviorism. The chief contribution of the
humanist to the study of anthropology is that he can
direct attention to human phenomena in terms of their
experientiality. Such a student strives to apprehend
phenomena in terms of their intrinsic, unique, constitutive qualities instead of in terms of such extrinsic and
alien considerations as their quantities and functions.

So the humanistic anthropologist, ranging over the
textures, the sounds, the tempo of Yoruba life, viewed
against the background of what his attentions to the
affecting presence have revealed to him, suggests to the
social anthropologist that energy is surging from the
wellspring of Yoruba life. He suggests that in ways either
obscure or plain, primeness and continuity of energy,
among other features, are enacted in and constitute the
experiential base of those aspects of culture that have
traditionally concerned the social anthropologist. Perhaps a careful examination of the respects in which the
font of energy nourishes the affecting presence will not
only be suggestive of the strategies and ends of such
analyses but also will lead us nearer to an understanding
of the nature of the cultural source.

2

The Aesthetic of Energy

The response to the limitations and needs I have described is that perspective upon the work "of art" which I have called *the affecting presence*, which as we have seen is a direct and immediate presentation, brought into being by culturally necessary and sufficient conditions of consciousness; these are the spatio-temporal disciplines and values, the media which these inform, and the aboutness of the work. The affecting presence exists by virtue of an irresolvable dynamic of tension among these domains. The *work of art* is called an *affecting presence* in recognition of the fact that the quintessential and definitive quality of such a work is that it possesses *being*, of a sort and in such a fashion that it is more like a man than an object. This is to say that in encounter with a witness it charges the occasion with all the force of its own presence, of its own intrinsic and electric qualities of self, and in its own terms. That with which one has this kind of encounter is *not* an object.

Certainly in its role in our lives the affecting presence is neither treated nor regarded as an object. On the contrary, it is everywhere—on at least some occasions during its existence—subject to the most careful and indeed expensive of attentions. There are in all probability very few recognized works of affecting presence in the world which are not better housed and more solicitously cared for than most of the people who constitute their publics—better, indeed, in many instances than the workers who created them. The affecting work is enshrined, honored when it dispenses saving grace and feared when it wreaks evil. To see that all these assertions are true we need only to look to the expensive structures and environments created for the purpose of providing a place in which to display such works. We need only to observe the enraptured audiences that gather awestruck to witness them; only to count the treasures and to note the honor accorded statues of Christian virgins or African ancestors; only to perceive the fear which attends the work that can manage evil, as among the Senufo for example who have a work, kajéguélédia (plate 6), which is believed to focus a laser-like power of evil with which it can wither that person toward whom its power is directed.

The affecting work, we see from this, is a work that abides in value. Like those of a person, the values of the affecting work are intrinsic. And as the person is in some major respect identical with those values intrinsic to him, so also is the affecting presence. Even among those peoples for whom an affecting work is *in value*—in existence, as it were, indeed—only when it is suffused with power, power is yet intrinsic to the work. And if such a presence is sometimes without manifest power, sometimes with a little, and sometimes incandescent with it, this situation is not different from that of the human being himself who sometimes suffers deprivation while at other times he endures overwhelming floods of cosmic energy, becoming possessed or sanctified. The significance of a work is its value, and its value is what the work is—the extent to which it incarnates consciousness, both the primal consciousness of the culturally irreducible spatio-temporal terms, and the terms of its specific *aboutness*. All this is intrinsic to the affecting presence. Save possibly for the computer, which with its "values" intrinsic to it becomes a kind of person as well, other man-made works are not accorded that honorific treatment paid to the affecting presence.

If it is not an object, what then is the affecting work? Why it must be a subject, for a subject is a self, characterized by intrinsic value and with the ability to initiate and to enact value. The human subject has great latitude in this respect, while the affecting presence is restricted. Similarly, the human subject can change the character or the field of his enacted value, while the affecting presence cannot. In contrast with the human, then, the affecting work is limited; we are therefore to view it as a limited subject.

Yet we cannot in any sense think of the affecting work as a full person, even though it shares many attributes with a person—indeed it is a person arrested at a moment in the continuous flux of his being—even down to the possession of both role and status. Aside from the evident reasons why we cannot regard the affecting presence fully as a person, there is a less obvious but critical further reason, which is that it lacks any possibility of the volition which is characteristic of the person—the ability to do what one will, to establish goals and subsequently to achieve them. The work that manages power, like the kajéguélédia, it must be remembered, is directed by a human agency.

Then is there that unique and critical property of

living beings, the power of exerting their unique, personal selves. They have *presence*, intrinsic identity and force. Since this is precisely the case with the affecting work, we thus call it the affecting presence, the modificand denoting its ontology and the modifier the special domain of it suasion.

The affecting presence is the delivering of a moment of the being of culture and of self into dynamic stasis, by means of establishing in the affecting presence those very conditions and ramifications of consciousness which the artist believes ought, by virtue of their particular value, to be externalized and made self-sufficient in the world. The affecting presence, then, is a projection *of* consciousness *in* consciousness. It is thus a direct presentation of the artist's shaped and meaningful awareness; it is not a symbol of that awareness. This is why the affecting presence is a force, a limited subject endowed with personality and inherent value, because it is in fact the most human of human estates incarnated into media which are no more alien to it than the cells and corpuscles that make up our bodies are alien to our breath and being, our bodies that in our daily lives incarnate our consciousness.

The affecting presence dictates the specific conditions of consciousness under which we apprehend it. Thus also is it a subject, initiating psychic action and dictating both the form and consequence that are the appropriate reaction to itself. The affecting presence cannot but be seen as a *process* of consciousness, one which—unlike a brief exposure to a person in the context of some random segment of a through-time engagement where wholeness is the result only of a long term definition—has wholeness of instant disclosure. It wholly possesses in its enactment the totality of its historical shape.

Although I have already briefly mentioned the spatio-temporal determinants or parameters of the work as being generic expressions of the cultural consciousness, I shall now develop the matter further. Consciousness we may take to be the sending and receiving of awareness which, like an immensely subtle and probing radar, fills all perceived outer and all imaginable inner space. Consciousness is, as the phenomenologists inform us, always directed; it has *intentionality*. We may infer from the existence of like-minded groups of people that it has certain general characteristics, or that people in the same groups direct their individual consciousnesses in similar ways. Culture, therefore, may be seen as a consensus of and in consciousness.

The irreducible schemata of centrifugality (called *extensionality*) and centripetality (called *intensionality*), and of continuity and discontinuity are the basic conditions in which consciousness exists. Indeed, I have postulated the existence of a continuum antecedent to this analysis of consciousness into spatial and temporal forms and have called that continuum of predisposition the *cultural metaphoric base*. This hypothetical base lies prior to temporal and spatial dimensions, causing all the affecting works of a given epoch or culture to enact common patterns. Without prior explicit analysis of the ways in which it would be achieved, there develops in any given period of a culture an affecting homogeneity of the arts irrespective of the physical differences among the media of their enactment. We can now see that the principle which quickens the cultural metaphoric base and justifies its postulation is a cultural consciousness, a formula for awareness which is basic to all perception and to all expression.

Neither Langer nor the traditional anthropologist has come face to face with this basic cultural fact and so, with respect to the appropriate perception of the real nature of the work of affecting presence, it seems to me, both have failed—the one to apprehend the distinctive nature of the affecting presence and the other its significance as a stasis of presented-consciousness-in-being. So it is not surprising that Langer loses the work between the media in which it exists and the mind which initiates it, that she can see the work only as a "virtual" reality, and so must necessarily conclude that the affecting work is not a presence but a symbol. She misses the pivotal point that the real medium of the affecting presence is consciousness, overtly and directly presented in the media which she maintains only *stand for* a further reality. Nor is it remarkable because of this failure, that the anthropologist, who has been greatly influenced by her work, has failed to understand the significance of works of affecting presence and has accordingly relegated them to an obscure position on the far periphery of those things relevant to an understanding of man.

The affecting media which support consciousness in its eventuation into the various forms of the affecting presence are surface, color, volume, tone, movement, work, situation, relationality, and experience. These are to be read strictly. Thus *color* should be understood to mean visual color and not tonal "color."

FORMAL
METAPHORS

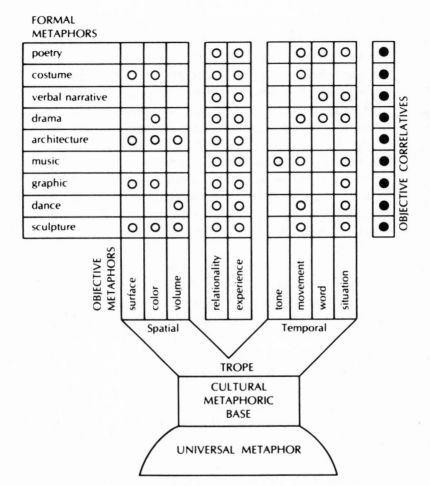

These media in Langer's view are the means by which
the nondiscursive symbol symbolizes, eventuating into
the virtual semblance of the logical structures of particular objects or events or states of affairs in the veritable
world. Such works, she would maintain, bear to the

veritable world the same relationship a formula bears
to reality. Thus is the Langerian nondiscursive symbol
a *formula for feeling*, and for her the media, with respect
to the whole work, become subsymbols each contribut-
ing its own bit to that complex which is the whole. On
Mrs. Langer's view, therefore, the media are the constit-
uents of the achieved "logical" structure of the nondiscursive symbol, and their function is to represent something which, apparently, is not intrinsic to the
nondiscursive symbol itself but rather to the transaction
between the one who makes and the one who perceives
the work.

Since the affecting presence, however, is of a nature
dramatically different from the nondiscursive symbol
in that it has no necessary demonstrative function but
rather is a presence in itself—enacting itself, celebrating
its own being—it follows that the media of the affecting
presence have as their function not representation but
presentation. The media of the affecting presence are
the minima of presentationality. They lie this side of
the basic cultural consciousness which they bear. The
real medium of the affecting presence therefore is consciousness itself, freighted into color, tone, volume,
surface, movement, word, and situation. Indeed, since
Mrs. Langer's nondiscursive symbol is to be seen as
mediating, rather than *presenting,* the affecting presence, which *presents,* must be *immediating.*[1] Thus we
ought to speak not of *media* but instead of *immedia.*

The immedia directly present our consciousness. They
create and extend the world and they do so in accordance

[1] Robert P. Armstrong, *The Affecting Presence; An Essay in Hu-*
manistic Anthropology (Urbana: University of Illinois Press, 1971),
p. 55.

with the permissions of the culture. When one makes an affecting presence one is not ordering the insignia of reality but rather the powers of a profound order of reality itself. He animates the inanimate with the electricity of living consciousness. It is for this reason that one is compelled to say when speaking of the artist's making of his unique work that he creates it, *creates* being that connotes the radiance, the wholeness, and the person-ality of his achievement.

Let us examine a work in order that we may see how it is that that intensive-continuity which I have argued characterizes the spatial forms of Yoruba sculpture, and which I now propose broadening to such an extent that it is to be seen as a primal state of Yoruba consciousness, is enacted by the constitutive immedia which bring about the particular texture and aboutness of the work.

The work I have chosen is a traditional mask called Epa (plate 7), one of a socially established genre of Yoruba masks of which Arnold Rubin has written:

> The meaning and function of the Epa masquerade varies considerably from place to place [in Ekiti]. A detailed report by Clarke ... on the ceremonies at Ora describes Epa as a great carver who has become the tutelary spirit of his people ... The dance is a twirling, leaping test of strength, since agility is prized and some of the masks weigh more than 100 pounds.
>
> The superstructure motifs vary widely, representing an extensive range of human and animal subjects. The stylized lower portion (IKOKO, "pot"), almost invariably janus-faced, remains relatively consistent; helmet masks of similar form are reported from a number of neighboring groups.

1. Sango Pedestal

2. Ose Sango

3. Ose Sango

4. Ose Sango

5. Ose Sango

6. Kajéguélédia

7. Epa mask, front

8.   Epa mask, back

9.   Epa mask, details

10.   Ogun axe

11. Ife head

12. Woman with twins

13.   Woman with twins, back

14. Woman with twins, side

15. Ogun axe, side

16. Ogun axe, detail

17.   Offertory piece with crocodiles

18.   Ogun axe, back

19.   Goya, *Prison Scene*

20.   Staff, front

21.　Staff, back

22.   Bronze pieces from Oro Society, front (21 inches)

23.   Bronze piece from Oro Society, side

Stylistic relationships are inadequately understood, but the configuration may have originated in the typical Yoruba practice of devotees carrying shrine carvings on their heads in festival processions.[2]

There is about the whole mask, but about the chief figure in particular, a decided hauteur, eventuating from the sculptor's careful adherence to the formal and affective dictates of the work itself respecting the presentation of a devotee. In some measure the work's hauteur derives from the careful composition of the face, with its relaxed yet dignified expression. At the same time, and in some further measure, its scale, which is impressive with the central figure towering over the secondary figures of the attendant and the sacrificial cock, is also important. So is its relationship to gravity, which is that of the tree's. This is to say that the figure is progressively the more released the farther it removes from the base that constitutes its earth. Thus the work swells as it soars with the result that inevitably and irrespective of one's own greater size, the witness feels as if he were looking up to the dominating, quiescent central figure. When worn atop the head, the mask argues this point even more authoritatively.

But while the sculpture expands as it soars, it does so with an energy that is, while subtle, nonetheless abundant. It is by no means the case that there is any meaningful violation of what is clearly a rigorously asserted imperative to preserve the vertical integrity of the actual tree from which the work was created. The

---

[2] Arnold Rubin, "Yoruba Sculpture in Los Angeles Collections," Montgomery Art Center, Exhibition Catalogue, Pomona College, p. 36.

sculpture, then, obeys the same dynamic laws as the tree itself—*in this respect*. In respect of the principle of brachiation *into space*, as the limbs of the tree do, the sculpture deviates from the law of the tree it has cannibalized. It is for this reason that one observes a scrupulous avoidance of the dramatic, affecting extension of the body into any space save that vertical one required for its intrinsic necessity to soar. This is notably true in terms of the avoidance of lateral extension—or to put the matter somewhat more positively, the mask is created in terms of the *assertion of lateral intension*.

Frontally and dorsally it may appear as though extension were to be seen as having been affectingly executed, for is it not the case that frontally the breasts and dorsally (plate 8) the buttocks and the feet extend beyond that imperious central volume of the work? It can only be replied that such extrusions into space do indeed occur; but whether these are to be seen as the deliberate violation of the figure's intensionality toward the end of achieving a dramatic, affecting exploitation of horizontal extension into space is quite another question. Certainly it cannot be maintained that this is so with the buttocks, which are minimal, and the feet, where it is clear that the sculptor intended and so carved them that their extension should be strikingly curtailed. The only question therefore concerns frontal extension. Certainly the breasts of the chief figure extend markedly into space. Yet it is difficult to argue that they significantly dissipate the intensionality of the whole work.

What is required is some definition of *extensionality* and, conversely, of *intensionality*, but any attempt at formulation cannot be marked by a high degree of precision. I would propose that a dancing Siva, with one leg and multiple arms extended—with even its fingers executed so as to exploit maximal extension into space—is an undeniable instance of extensionality. It is indeed at the outer limit of the possibility of extension. The Siva reaches toward that circumference maximally conceivable for it. But is it in any sense true of the Epa mask that it too reaches toward such a circumference? Or is it not rather the case that there is inherent in the work a clear indication that the purpose is to adhere to the economical discipline of the core stated as a theme by the mask's helmet and by the platform upon which the figures rest? This definition of the core is never significantly violated, neither by the secondary figures nor by the breasts of the main figure.

The sublimation of even the slightest whim of formal vagary to the resolute re-enactment of the core results simultaneously in the achievement of two basic affecting conditions: intension and continuity. The former, as we have seen, is brought about by means of the inhibition of horizontal or lateral extension into space. Continuity on the other hand derives not only from the determination to enact the core but also, and perhaps even more, from the dramatic emphasis given the long lines of the work and from the creation and exploitation through repetition of certain motifs which are to be found in it. Consider as a most striking instance of this motif-repetition the prevalence of eyes, for surely what engages one greatly in the total work is not only the presence of the figure as a towering presence, but also and simultaneously one is aware how the eyes dominate in both the face of the mask (Ikoko) and the faces of the figures, each constituting a dramatic restatement of the other. Further, the knees and the tips of the breasts play a variation upon this theme, enhancing the upward, continuous soar of the work. Needless to say the eyes of the cock and the attendant female figure, as well as the complementary forms of the cock's wattles and body and the human figure's sacrificial offering, also make their singular and complementary contributions to this phenomenon of continuity by means of the great frequency with which occurs a primary motif and its thematic variations. This approach to the execution of a line through the perpetration of numerous points is of course the same approach to the presentation of a mass as that employed by the Pointilists.

In his witnessing of that act which is the work, one notes also the remarkable designs which help create its surface. Those designs cover the back, the breasts, the abdomen, and the arms of the central figure, and the sole theme of the design is the triangle (plate 9), executed in white and red. One is struck with two additional facts of these designs—first, perhaps, that they enjoy a strong outline, the sharp definition of one element with respect to the other; but he notices subsequently as he learns to perceive the whole that the individual triangles join to form larger ones. The design also, therefore, emphasizes the pointilistic or atomistic approach to the creation of continuity! One should also note that the motif for the overall body design is set by the triangular pieces which in part comprise the necklace worn by the main figure.

And yet there is more—there is that vertical system built on a leitmotif of circles which gives both pronounced interest and variety to the work, subtly accentuating its thrust by reminding one of its happening

and at the same time lending accentuation to the
three-dimensionality, the coreness, and the wholeness
of the work. There can be little doubt that this theme
enjoys its primary presentation in the base of the helmet
and in the disc which constitutes the figures' earth, that
it is restated in the form of the helmet which is the
mask itself, is played with in the forehead line which
play is in turn itself restated in the counterpose of the
downward drooping belt (plate 7). The main presentation occurs once again in the necklace and in the
undercutting which is the line of the jaw and the chin.
The ridgings of the coiffure and the final paradoxical
thrust of the central ridge running at right angles to
these constitute the motif's coda. The circular system
thus embraces the vertical ones, not only confining
them, enhancing their continuity, but both commencing
the work at the bottom of the mask and finishing it
with its brisk and definitive finial. All of these considerations are of dynamics and thus pertain to the work's
system of energies.

We have progressed from a consideration of the inten-
sively continuous existence of the Epa mask as a spatial
form to the intensive-continuity of systems of structural
and design motifs which exist as of a different order.
These are compounded of the sculptural immedia of
volume and surface. The surface is further characterized,
however, by an overall coating so that it is of homogeneous texture; and there is marked homogeneity of the
restrained chroma of the colors used, which asserts both
intension and continuity. The Epa mask now exists for
us, a thing in itself, fully born into our consciousness!
If at first, because of the possibility of its strangeness
to our perceptions, we perceived it as static, we now

see it alive, a dynamic complex of carefully interrelated systems which devolve upon and involve one another in the energies of its own universe.

In proclaiming intension and continuity—by means of an atomistic constitution—the work does not symbolize. (What could it possibly symbolize? There is no known referent.) The spatial form and the immedia do not symbolize, they *embody* actual conditions of form and process which we may presume to be at least significant terms or conditions within the Yoruba consciousness.

The incarnation of consciousness into physical properties in the immedia constitutes the ground for the only hypothesis capable of satisfactorily accounting for the unique characteristics of the affecting work as viable in its inalienable estate as *presence*. That this is the case, however, can be firmly understood only upon the basis of a fuller understanding of how it is that the media incarnate consciousness to become immedia.

Let us now invoke this aesthetic of energy in order to ascertain whether we can apprehend through it a further instance of immedia bearing consciousness—in ways we might otherwise neglect to see, or through devices and conventions we might very well perceive but which make little or no sense to us, striking us instead perhaps as merely bizarre. Since I have already demonstrated how an aesthetic of energy exists among the Yoruba, it is now my deeper purpose to reveal a tight structure of consciousness permeating the total being of the work—through form, through content, through the simultaneous and inextricable realization of both via the immedia.

It is true that we could consider the Epa mask further,

but the sculpture I have chosen for analysis in terms of this experimental model of an aesthetic of energy is an axe for Ogun in the form of a hyrax-mounting man (plate 10). The axe measures 20 inches in height, 1 1/2 inches in frontal width, 4 inches in lateral, exclusive of the blade, which is 6 inches long and 6 3/4 inches high. Aside from these details, and the fact that it is superbly carved, I know nothing more about the piece. It is obvious that it is a work that is quintessentially Yoruba. It is therefore a marvelous piece for study. I regard it as quintessentially Yoruba because it is as richly a created network as one might easily imagine of those energy processes that quicken the Yoruba affecting work into that switched-on circuit of energy which is a presence.

It is possible I suppose that there might be some who might maintain that the piece is too Yoruba—too rich, too intensional, too markedly demanding existence through its heady metabolism of lavish metaphors. I myself do not believe this, seeing the work instead as a masterpiece in the exercise of that rare degree of control which can with confidence bring a work close to excess in nearly every respect and yet with breath-taking virtuosity stop short. Indeed, it is the profligacy of labor and of imagination abundantly spent upon this work, stopping before that point at which its energy would have been dissipated in the pointless expenditures of the rococo, which elevates the piece into the ranks of the superb. It is its careful flirtation with excess which, echoing the primeness of energy, argues the validity of the whole work.

The case is very much the same with the intricately engraved surface, a surface which while unusual in the

Yoruba corpus is certainly not unknown. Indeed it immediately occurs to one that this treatment finds antecedence in those ancient life heads, whose surfaces are as intricately traced (plate 11); and a like richness is to be seen in the scarification of the breast and the back of an offertory piece depicting a woman with twins (plates 12, 13, 14), as well as in the surface decoration of the Epa mask we have already studied (plate 9). In none of these instances is the work more elaborate, however, than it is on the Ogun axe. But the careful use of plain surfaces—the eyes, ears, and nose, the arms and hands, the flute, the legs and the feet, the janus faces—once again saves the work from excess. As a result of their rich context, what strength these plain areas achieve! Such sure control removes the work from the dangers of self-indulgence. The abundant energy of the work is conserved.

But let us look in an orderly fashion at the various energy systems of the work, concentrating our attentions first upon the processes of continuity and intension. The long-line development of the work is dramatically achieved, not only in the top-to-bottom realization of the work—a handle topped by a janus-head that bears to the supporting column almost the classical proportions of head-to-body relationships, but also in the surmounting figure of Ogun, which from frontal perspective has only continuity (plate 10), with the theme of over-all continuity independently restated in the legs, the flute, and the nose. In fact there is a contrapuntal and complementary system of continuity-constituting details: the fingers gripping the flute curve fully around it, and, from the lateral view (plate 15), relate to the serifs of plain bands which periodically encircle the figure. From this same lateral view, it is readily to be seen that here too continuity enjoys extraordinary development. Indeed all one can say of the work's intensionality is that it is so subjected to the achievement of continuity that intensionality can only be said to be total. The energy expressed in the work, in the full, is not in the least subtracted by one extensive line! The continuity of contained energy thus finds in this work absolute metaphoric incarnation.

It is fascinating that the sculptor of this work used both of the means available to him to achieve continuity—both the long lines of linearism and the particle-density of atomism, which is the principle of the realization of continuity employed in Yoruba temporal forms of narration, music, and dance, and which we also see used to create the designed surface of the Epa mask. Continuity by atomism is achieved chiefly by the rich density of the engraving which covers the whole work, and by the larger pattern areas which these surface details create.

The energy of balance eventuates from the fact that, with respect to the parameters of intensionality and continuity, the maximization of intensionality at the same time maximizes balance as well. Otherwise, energy exists in the system of twos—the double row of cowries at the base, the janus heads, and the pair of animals (plates 10, 16). The animals face opposite directions; and of the janus heads, one is that of an old man while the other is that of a youth, a powerful apposition which, by bracketing a life span between two heads, achieves continuity through complementarity. This careful use of balance through complementary appositions is not unknown in other Yoruba works. Consider for example

the reversed position of the alligators in the superb
screen enclosing a votive figure in the offertory piece
(plate 17). This kind of balance asserts the eternal
process of alternation that characterizes the nature of
the energy process as the Yoruba perceive it—alternation
between life and death, flow and ebb, prime and diminution.

While there may be narrative dimensions I am missing, nonetheless in terms of processes, the energy of
compressed balance derives from the three-way col-
lapsed pun which constitutes the dorsal aspect of the
axe (plate 18). In the first of these, we perceive the tail
of the surmounting animal, the tail of Ogun's cap, and
the head of the mounted animal. The first pun upon
this configuration is that the head of the mounted
animal (a hyrax) constitutes the tip of the tail of Ogun's
cap. The second pun is that the cap is naught but the
elongation of the animal's tail.

Paradox is presented in the very use, simultaneously,
of the linear and atomistic achievements of continuity
which I have already commented upon, a fact which
suggests the *illusion* of apparent differences—all to be
resolved with reference to the oneness of cosmic energy,
which suggests that "paradox" is to be understood meta-
phorically, as a dramatic device juxtaposing various
phases of likes and not of unlikes. The fact that here,
as elsewhere in the work one aspect performs more than
one metaphoric function attests to the marvelous economy of the piece and so to its dramatic force, its rich
and concentrated energies.

The entire work is hyperbolic—it is, as we have already
noted, quintessentially Yoruba, a fact which is in itself
a hyperbole. The dual achievement of its continuity also

constitutes a hyperbole, and the fact that this duality also forms both compressed metaphor and a paradox is yet an additional paradox, and that a further compressed metaphor. It is as though the work stood among mirrors, reflecting and counter-reflecting its energy system to brilliant, clearly echoing infinity! And the reduction of intension to such a point that there is no extension whatsoever is clearly hyperbolic as well. As for the creation of energy by means of repetition, we need only to look to the system of the appearance of twos and to the intricately repeated motif of engraving which constitutes the surface.

As a result of this complex system of metaphoric processes, marvelously economically achieved by means of multiple metaphoric roles for each feature, the work becomes a masterfully vital example of the Yoruba baroque at its best—ever controlled, ever radiant with energy. These incarnations of energy are not, however, restricted to spatial forms, but may be seen in temporal forms as well.

We can see the same conditions and dynamics prevailing in an affecting work in words. In order to demonstrate this, I have chosen Amos Tutuola's *The Palm-Wine Drinkard*.[3] This work, Tutuola's first, is surely one of the most discussed works of African literature, a fact which testifies to its magnetism, which is one of the chief vital properties of an affecting work. *The Palm-Wine Drinkard* is a fast-paced work which presents the search of a prodigious drinkard of palm-wine for his palm-wine tapster who has been killed in the exercise of his duties. It is a moving book, a funny book,

[3] Amos Tutuola, *The Palm-Wine Drinkard* (New York: Grove Press, paper, 1962).

a beautiful book; it is also a rich and hence a seminal
book. This last and particularly telling factor is demonstrated by the impact Tutuola has had on at least two
gifted artists, Twins Seven-Seven and Adebisi Fabunmi.
However, it is not my purpose here to argue Tutuola's
genius, but rather only to show in his work the operation
of the Yoruba imagination in terms of achieving via the
metaphors I have identified that aesthetic, or more
properly, that ontology of energy whose existence I have
hypothesized.

Some general consideration must first be given to the
nature of metaphor in that affecting presence which
exists in language. While one accepts without confusion
the idea of metaphor as processive incarnation in the
other affecting forms, when it comes to literature the
fact that there is a special meaning already attached
to the term "metaphor" throws an almost Tutuolan
obstacle before us. It is important to realize, therefore,
that metaphor is a process by means of which the artist
creates in various spatial and temporal media states of
affective being, states which, once established, are forever thereafter independent of either creator or witness.
Thus it is that in the following discussion I shall treat
metaphor as the mode of affecting existence of the verbal
affecting presence and not significantly as those discrete
language phenomena which are in traditional critical
discourse called "metaphors."

In the temporal arts of the Yoruba action is achieved
atomistically, by which I mean that a continuum of
actional or narrative surface is created by means of a
rich density of discrete actions, whether these be geneti-
cally related, as they are in a fastpaced spy thriller,
or merely contiguous, as is the case in *The Palm-Wine*

Drinkard. "Action-packed," a cliche which is so common to the westerner that he hardly perceives that condition any more, describes the prevalent state of *The Palm-Wine Drinkard.* We are so inured, indeed, that we must overcome some of our world-weariness and perceive afresh if we are adequately to witness that affecting surface of continuing engagement and re-engagement which creates this work's atomistic continuity. But continuity is achieved as well by means of other dynamics—by means of constancy of narrator, even though his physical form is subject to instant metamorphosis; by means of a uniformly bizarre world in which the action is set; by means of a constant theme; by means of a pervasion of highly generalized characters and events; and finally by means of a continuum of compressed metaphor, to which I shall subsequently give some attention.

In narrative, as in any temporal form, atomic change is the basic dynamic and so it is the irreducible metaphor of energy The narrative exists only when, like energy, it is characterized by full and vital flow. The character of the energy incarnated, therefore, is a direct function of the rate and complexity of actional change. In *The Palm-Wine Drinkard* the rate of change is frequent and the pace therefore swift. Change, however, is not a function solely of scene or action change, but comes about also as a function of alterations in the substantive and the metaphoric continua. Thus most incidents are event-packed, many of them tend to be brief, they involve many physical and emotional dimensions (fear, wonder, color, transformation) and every metaphoric process. Every variable upon which the achievement of the work depends is subject to change, and by these means is the change rich and complex, making the work's charge of energy so as well. These variables, in their interrelated and interdigitated reciprocals of change, create a continuum of narrative energy as vibrantly and in much the same way as the multi-drums of an ensemble create continuous musical energy.

The Palm-Wine Drinkard exploits not only continuity but intensionality as well. Marked individualization of characters, and concomitantly of their actions is a means by which extension is achieved in a work. The generalization of actor and action, it conversely follows, is inevitably a stratagem by means of which intension is brought about. The absence of significant interiority in the characters is yet another of the practices by which their generalization and, thus, intensionality eventuates, as also is the inhibition of the characters' status as subjects and the resulting minimization of their volition and their delivery over to forces over which they have little control. Indeed magic becomes the surrogate of free-will.

Intensionality is also achieved by means of a severe restriction of the range in kinds of situations which are developed and the kinds of resolutions to which they are subject. Thus highly generalized characters enact a continuum of rapidly changing but nonetheless generically similar events, and thus does Tutuola create a work whose primary space-time existence is a direct metaphoric realization of the two basic parameters of energy. In all this lies the metaphoric significance of atomism and intension when viewed in terms of a model oriented toward an ontology of energy—this is the pulse of being, asserted by the complex continuity of *The Palm-Wine Drinkard*, endowed with force by full intensionality, as the continuity of water through a hose gains force by means of restriction.

It is not only intension and continuity, however, which generate the energy that is *The Palm-Wine Drinkard*. Its dynamism is presented through the energy systems of complementarity, hyperbole, and repetition, and it generates the primeness of energy as well, through ephebism and "sacrifice."

The Palm-Wine Drinkard is, from beginning to end, a bravura enactment in the primeness of energy. The extraordinary resourcefulness of the ageless drinkard argues the unflaggable energies one would expect of a work presenting the primeness of energy through ephebism. And the restoration, or in the case of the existential continuum of a novel, the steady maintenance of maximal energy is accomplished by means of the incessant accretion of richly invented miraculous happenings. The wild energy of the miracle with commensurate luxuriance immeasurably enhances the energy of the work of which it is constitutive. Quick inventiveness and profligate imagination filter through the work's being and thus through our own, each bright luminosity, like a struck match, consuming itself so that the whole may persist in radiance.

Complementarity is a dominant order of energy in the work, complementarity through balance, through paradox, and through compressed metaphor, which of all the means is perhaps the most richly employed, the most pervasive, and the most effective.

Compressed metaphor, since the work is a fully actualized one, lies at its heart, pervading its entirety. The compressed metaphor of the work is to be found in the nature of the palm-wine drinkard himself. Is he merely a man with a prodigious thirst, a god—indeed the father of the gods—a powerful juju man, a culture hero? He is at one and the same time, and to some extent, all of these. He is multiply endowed, and one can never tell in advance which of his roles is going to dominate. As man, he suffers and fears; as a god, he can do all; as a powerful juju man, he can divert events which would otherwise certainly destroy him. As a culture hero, a role more asserted by Western than by African critics, his affairs tend to assume vast import. The palm-wine drinkard is a compressed metaphor of human, prodigious, divine, and magical energies.

There are also lesser orders of compressed metaphor which energize the work. An example of this is to be found in the incident entitled "On our way to the Unreturnable-Heaven's Town" in which we can uncomfortably experience frustrated physical energy, deprivation, constraint, and anguish—all in all a markedly kinetic experience.

> After that, they took us to a wide field which was in the full heat of the sun, there were no trees or shadow near there and it was cleared as a football field; it was near the town. Then they dug two pits or holes side by side, in size of which would reach the jaw of a person, in the centre of the field. After that they put me into one and my wife into the second and replaced the earth that they had dug out and pressed it hard in such a way that we could hardly breathe. Then they put food near our mouths, but we were unable to touch or eat it; they knew that we were very hungry by that time. And after that, the whole of them cut whips and began to flog our heads, but we had no hands to defend our heads. At last they brought an eagle before us

to take out our eyes with its beak, but the eagle was simply looking at our eyes, it did no harm to us.[4]

There are also instances of compressed verbal metaphors, for those who wish their metaphors comfortably to exist in words:

> ... that they had nearly caught me or if I continued to run away like that, no doubt, they would catch me sooner, then I changed the lady to a kitten and put her inside my pocket and changed myself to a very small bird which I could describe as a "sparrow" in English language.[5]

This example is also illustrative of the process of paradox, in the work's *being*. Indeed, events of this sort are the source of the energy of paradox in the work. As a matter of fact, the very existence of our prodigious tippler is in the nature of a paradox.

Molara Ogundipe asserts that Tutuola has given

> *The Palm-Wine Drinkard* an asymmetric form thereby increasing the dramatic impact of his tale. Roughly twenty-one episodes make up the Departure ... that is, the journey to Deads' Town, five bring him back to the river which all too frequently in folk imagination demarcates the land of the dead from the land of the living and about four episodes comprise the events taking place after his return (from his Quest). Twenty-one episodes lead us suspensefully to Deads' Town ... nine bring us back hurriedly as they should, to the original scene to which place our interest is now riveted. We would not have had the patience to go through too many

[4] Ibid., p. 61.
[5] Ibid., p. 28.

episodes on the return journey. The overall structure of *The Palm-Wine Drinkard* is therefore pleasing.[6]

The point is well taken. There *is* an energy to asym-
metry, though the opposite form is in general the
characteristic energy process of the works of the Yoruba.

In any case, there is at least one major symmetry
in the work we must not neglect to mention, a symmetry
of the whole. The whole work exists as a frame, that
is it exists between the enclosing actions which occur
in his home village before he leaves and after he returns
to his home, on both of which occasions he gives himself
over to providing feasting for all his parasitic friends.
In between are all the rich experiences in the great world
of the Yoruba imagination as incarnated by Tutuola.
One part ends with the visit to the Unreturnable-
Heaven's Town, which is the nadir of his experience of
suffering. Throughout all the incidents of the first part
the drinkard is father of the gods. In the second part
he actually achieves his goal, the encounter with his
dead tapster in the Deads' Town, all this time protected
by his immortality, attained in the opening incident of
this part. The two parts stand to each other in the
relationship of balance by complementarity, for the
second part ends with the locale and situation with
which the first began. As we have seen, this is not an
uncommon metaphoric means of the works of the Yoruba affecting universe.

Hyperbole is of the essence of the book and thus there
is not one scene nor one being in it drawn in ordinary

[6] Molara Ogundipe, "*The Palm-Wine Drinkard*—A Re-Assessment,"
p. 25, pp. 22-26, *Ibadan*, No. 28, July, 1970.

scale. Let me more for delight than argument cite Tutuola's creation of one of his hyperbolic monsters.

> ... we saw a "Spirit of Prey," he was big as hippo-
> potamus, but he was walking upright as a human-
> being; his both legs had two feet and tripled his
> body, his head was just like a lion's head and every
> part of his body was covered with hard scales, each
> of these scales was the same in size as a shovel or
> hoe, and all curved towards his body. If this "Spirit
> of Prey" wanted to catch his prey, he would simply
> be looking at it and stand in one place, he was not
> chasing his prey about, and when he focused the
> prey well, then he would close his large eyes, but
> before he would open his eyes, his prey would be
> already dead and drag itself to him at the place
> that he stood. When this "Spirit of Prey" came
> nearer to the place where we slept on that night,
> he stood at about 80 yards away from us, and looked
> at us with his eyes which brought out a floodlight
> like mercury in colour.[7]

Energy by means of repetition is common—not only in the repeated patterns of involvement and extrication which compose the actional pattern of the work, but in its rhetoric as well. I shall illustrate this with two famous examples.

> ... they laughed at us if bombs explode, and we
> knew "Laugh" personally on that night, because
> as every one of them stopped laughing at us,
> "Laugh" did not stop for two hours. As "Laugh"
> was laughing at us on that night, my wife and myself
> forgot our pains and laughed with him, because he

[7] Tutuola, *Drinkard*, p. 54.

was laughing with curious voices that we never heard before in our life. We did not know the time that we fell into his laugh, but we were only laughing at "Laugh's" laugh and nobody who heard him when laughing would not laugh, so if somebody continue to laugh with "Laugh" himself, he or she would die or faint at once for long laughing, because laugh was his profession and he was feeding on it.[8]

My wife had said of the woman we met: "She was not a human-being and she was not a spirit, but what was she?" She was the Red-smaller-tree who was at the front of the bigger Red-tree, and the bigger Red-tree was the Red-king of the Red-people of Red-town and the Red-bush and also the Red-leaves on the bigger Red-tree were the Red-people of the Red-town in the Red-bush.[9]

In sum, *The Palm-Wine Drinkard* enacts primordial affecting space and time, primeness and dynamism in terms of the same processes of metaphorization as the Ogun axe. By means of these processes energy is simultaneously both created and conserved. The awareness of this work's energy is not unique to this present writer. Obiechina states, "In Kafka's stories, metamorphosis is a process of de-energization ... Tutuola emphasizes the dignity and vital energy of the human kind."[10]

There is evidence in Yoruba sculpture and literature, as the examples we have studied demonstrate, to support the hypothesis that *energy* is the informing principle of the Yoruba cultural metaphoric base, as William Fagg

[8] Ibid., pp. 46-47.
[9] Ibid., p. 83.
[10] E. N. Obiechina, "Amos Tutuola and the Oral Tradition," pp. 85-106, 88-89, *Presence Africaine,* LXV, 1968.

suspected. Contrary to Fagg's suspicion, however, the dynamics inherent in the actualization of energy *are* of distinct and particular consequence. We perceive in the Yoruba affecting presence—in sculpture and literature, at least—the direct metaphoric realization of the characteristics of energy, which is to say its continuity and its primeness as a principle in the constitution of the work. Further we discern as well in the Yoruba affecting presence a dense and deep fabric of metaphoric processes productive of energy—complementarity (through balance, paradox, and compressed metaphor), hyperbole, and repetition. We may therefore consider our hypothesis as probable, though there is no reason to presume that energy is *exclusively* the informing principle or that it is so in terms *necessarily* as simple as those indicated here.

But in so enacting energy, *what* precisely are these works doing? The answer to this is quite simple: they are enacting the very shape and energy of the Yoruba consciousness. By such means the works eventuate. Such shapes and processes are themselves immedia of the works, using word, wood, and iron as life uses the body. And so it is that by enacting the cultural consciousness of space, time, and energy, and by asserting these in particularly concentrated fashion in behalf of and in the terms of the aboutness of the works, so it is that a celebration of consciousness occurs. This celebration of consciousness becomes a particularly apt metaphorical realization in the case of the axe, with surface intension, continuity, aboutness, and dynamics conveying intense focus and force in and of consciousness.

The cultural consciousness inexorably makes the primordial, the *basic* declaration of the work. Within this

that subsequential aspect of consciousness which is the
aboutness of the work eventuates as a particular realization (the general realization of consciousness existing
explicitly only to the perception of the ethno-aestheti-
cian). So it is that Yoruba consciousness asserts its
cultural reality in terms of centripetality, continuity,
and a special kind of energy. All cultures are endowed
with their inexorable and primal consciousness—the
point of departure and arrival, as in the affecting
presence. Thus are the shape and the process of consciousness in their utter primacy *given*, and so is their
givenness a *sine qua non* of culture.

3

Consciousness and Attentionality

This clear givenness lends an inevitability to the affecting presence, deriving from the fact that it is natural to man's world. Further, as one encounters a man so, much in the same fashion, does he encounter the affecting presence since both are construed of consciousness and since both fix their witnesses with their own attentions in return for those he directs to them. Man and the affecting presence are thus, in this basic stratum of their being *consubstantial*. And the affecting presence itself is an event of probity, as compelling as man. We perceive with a shock of recognition that the affecting presence with respect to which we stand in witness exists not only in its own terms but also in our own terms as well! The affecting presence, once created, once witnessed, is as given as its witness because it shares with him the same unquestionable ground, being in consciousness—the affecting presence only emanating, the witness both emanating and receiving the electricity of consciousness.

This electrical givenness of consciousness makes it possible for one to ask questions and to make hypotheses about its operation but at the same time makes it impossible even to contemplate the possibility of suspending it, to imagine a raw world unprobed by it,

unattended by its focusing power of apprehending
aliveness. It is, in short, inconceivable that one might
place oneself anterior to consciousness in order to perceive it as a phenomenon. Further, one knows consciousness only in particular instances, never in general.

Consciousness is given in basic cultural terms which
are both inexorable and of nearly inscrutable subtlety,
such that they persist even (indeed, perhaps *especially*)
when one does not know that they are doing so. In order
to demonstrate this fact, I shall consider the contemporary painting "Ogogoro Man in an Intoxicated
Dream" by Oshogbo artist Twins Seven-Seven, which
is printed across from the title page of this book.

To be sure, there was some painting in the tradition:
for example sculptures, as we have already seen, were
polychromed; and in some instances the walls of build-
ings were painted with figures and with designs. But
these few activities present nothing of the scope, the
seriousness, or the probing of the works of a few of the
artists from Oshogbo who, in contrast with the traditional artists (who work in the terms of a clearly defined
inventory of socially approved classes), are to be considered *studio artists*, devoting themselves to more greatly
individuated kinds of *self* expression than tended to be
the case within the tradition. Along with this—indeed
in order to bring this end about—they are dedicated to
a high degree of technical and compositional invention.
Despite the fact that this energetic experimentation is
characteristic of them, however—and notably among
them Twins Seven-Seven—it is also true that these
artists are profoundly Yoruba.

But within the tradition, by and large, two-dimen-
sionality tends to be avoided. Even in beadwork (which
is reasonably common, being used for pouches, for

crowns, and for the handles of some utensils) three-dimensional figures are themselves often beaded and affixed to the surface. Indeed the crowns of Yoruba kings are characteristically enriched with beaded animals—chameleons, notably—and plants. Thus, often beadwork is less two dimensional than sculptural. Further, the traditional painting is executed either from a palette restricted to earth colors, as we have seen from our study of the Epa mask, or from a hectic one of a few quite electric primary colors. In contrast, the palette of Twins Seven-Seven is both wider and more carefully controlled. Finally, "Ogogoro Man" exists as a unified composition, in contrast with traditional Yoruba works of situational intent. In the tradition, situations are executed primarily in doors carved in relief and in the more complex of the Epa masks. Both are characterized by a high degree of episodicism which suggests the Yoruba narrative. Even in the case of the simpler Epa masks, where such episodes do not constitute the work, as in the Epa considered here, there is a one-two-threeness—a discreteness—about the figures in their relationships one to the other which is not found in the Twins Seven-Seven painting.

These are the respects in which this work diverges from the tradition. And yet the differences are more striking than they are important, for the respects in which the "Ogogoro Man" is rooted within the traditional aesthetic are more numerous and, I think, more interesting than the ways in which it deviates from that traditional aesthetic. Certainly they are more significant in terms of the demonstration of my point about the intransigent persistence of culture as a principle of consciousness.

Let us consider first the painting's crowded busyness.

We instantly recognize this as an incarnation of the Yoruba energy we have already discussed and which we shall consider further. Then let us direct our attentions to that ornate background which seems somehow familiar, despite the undeniable fact of its novelty. This compelling familiarity is attributable to the fact that we have already become acquainted with its generative principle: the achievement of continuity, in this instance of background-world, by means of a density of recurring elements.

Once again, writing to the issue of continuity, observe the face of the drunk and dreaming man. Familiarly we note his over-large eyes, and the prominence accorded the nose, two factors which as in the case of the sculpture conspire to create of the face a continuum for sense. Also again the body of the man soars, as does that of the chief sculptured figure of the Epa mask, becoming greater in size the farther it is removed from the gravity of its earth. Straight lines are not emphasized, and thus in contrast with the sculpture cannot be considered as a means to the achievement of continuity; but on the other hand, the lines are as long as possible. In any event, the points of articulation tend to be de-emphasized so that flow, which is the force of continuity, is achieved. In this respect I call to attention not so much the man's right arm as his left, his knees, his fingers, and his toes. Note also the structural oversimplification of the wings of the flying creatures whose complexity is subordinated in order that the continuity of the wings' surfaces might gain stronger rendition.

The continuity this piece presents is reinforced by the most important aspect of the painting's intensionality, namely its use of carefully related colors. But though the palette of Twins Seven-Seven is wider than that used by the painter of the Epa mask, it is not very wide. It still reflects the disciplining of intension, as it does also in the marked closeness of the colors one to another in both their chroma and their hue.

But how, it may be reasonably asked, can one speak further about the intensionality of a painting so numerously depicting birds, some of which are in full flight and all of which are endowed with such extraordinary beaks? In the first place, of course, it would be patently absurd to maintain that in an intensive work of art extension may not occur. Of course it may. Birds in flight obviously must have extended wings, and just as surely they must have beaks! The proper question then becomes one of relative emphasis. In this work the simple fact of the extension of the birds' wings is not a condition which greatly excites the painter, causing him to lavish much affecting or technical attention upon their execution. And while it is undeniably true that the beaks of the birds are extravagantly developed, it is also questionable whether such exaggeration is relatively any greater than that given the Ogogoro Man's nose, or that given to the eyes. Further that relationship to gravity which has a figure swell as it forms is here reduced to a convention so that the head is still greater even though all parts of the birds' bodies are, in flight at least, horizontally all related to gravity in the same degree. Thus it cannot be asserted that the admittedly exaggerated beak demonstrates any marked interest in extensionality. In any case, the in-tending of the birds' beaks en masse is striking—creating a strong centripetality in the work, detracted from only by the gaze of Ogogoro Man who dreamily looks down, though not beyond the boundaries of the work.

"Ogogoro Man in an Intoxicated Dream" presents

an intensive continuity and it achieves this by means of dynamic principles which are at work also in the presentation of the Epa mask. In this work intension is more clearly, though perhaps not more forcibly a process than in other works we have studied, with the greatest weight of the painting existing at the periphery, compelling a marked intending of energy toward the relatively quiet, focused-upon center. But it is the processes of continuity—complementarity and repetition—which are most familiar to us. This is evident in the atomistic background of nearly identically patterned flowers, in the intending of the variously sized but similarly designed birds. The force of hyperbole is most energetically asserted by the exaggerated features, by the nightmarish quality of the work's aboutness, by the very great force of its intension. This is but a ready gloss designed only to make clear the fact that despite the novelty of the work, *difference* at the cultural level is more apparent than real. What one witnesses here is not the accidental congruence of two styles but rather the suasion of a powerful Yoruba aesthetic whose basic principles beat deeply in the Yoruba consciousness and will not subside before the fortuitous presence of mere novelty.

The affecting presence is thus executed in deep accordance with imperatives existing beyond the explicit formulations of the conceptual mind. They are therefore implicit. And further, being imperatives, they are not arbitrary. So, aconceptual, implicit, and nonarbitrary, these imperatives are both compelling and organic. It is important to note that when we say of these imperatives that they are implicit and nonconceptual we identify the alternative to saying of them that they are "unconscious," which we cannot say if we are to say further that the ultimate medium of the affecting presence is consciousness itself. Thus the Yoruba drive toward atomistic intensive-continuity pervades from the far and nonverbal reaches of consciousness, being of the shape and the substance of consciousness. Why so much of the real shape of a culture lies unperceived by either indigene or anthropologist is precisely owing to the fact that it is a condition of consciousness from which the indigene cannot gain distance great enough to perceive it, and which may be sufficiently out of phase with the anthropologist's own grounding that unless he know this specifically and attempt to compensate for it he cannot perceive that culture save in terms of the grid of his own.

If the ultimate spatio-temporal terms in which the affecting presence exists are not arbitrary, then they are necessary. But in what sense are they necessary? The universality of affecting works suggests that consciousness is characterized at least in part by a need to electrify the external world with the dynamics of its own vitality, humanizing it after its own image. Thus does man make the world! And yet some cultures are characterized by a wealth and others by a paucity of affecting forms, so this need is by no means as undeniable as, let us say, the need for food. It is, however, perhaps man's most basic *human* need.

Thus man's consciousness is projected upon the world in fulfillment of a human requirement. But it also follows that such requirements can only be met in certain terms. Thus consciousness must be imposed upon the world in terms which are recognizable to it, which is to say its own terms. When we think to explain the power of the affecting presence, it is this very fact of its necessity that we must bear in mind and which lies deeply at the heart of that explanation. Since this necessity derives not from the fact that man is animal, but rather from the fact that he is human, it thus arises in his particularity. It is cultural and not biological.

It is a human imperative that consciousness be imposed upon the world; it is a cultural imperative that in a *particular* group of people *particular* patterns of knowing and feeling prevail. Since the world exists only when such impositions happen, consciousness and culture are at base identical. Indeed all anthropological descriptions of culture are merely hypostases of a consensual detritus of consciousness.

So it is an imperative of consciousness that it impose the order of itself upon the world in order that the world might come *to be* in meaningful, human terms. Naturally there is, the world over, a spectrum described by the various possibilities of realized forms, from those of the culture of one people to those of the culture of another. In any case, the individual consciousness enacts those patterns one perceives at the cultural level. The profound inevitability of the assertion of the Yoruba form of this consciousness is to be seen in the work of Twins Seven-Seven; apparently new, it yet enacts terms that are not only merely familiar but are in point of fact quintessential. It is only in the most superficial ways that his work seems at radical odds with his cultural tradition.

The necessary function of the affecting presence is to incarnate consciousness, freeing it to a life of its own in the world, liberating it from its customary prison in one's interiority in order that one's interiority may be superimposed upon the world about him in a particularly meaningful way. The work of affecting presence holds the mirror up—not to nature but to man. The world is caused to bear the supreme fact of man's presence in it. It is owing to this achieved end that the affecting presence is presentational. The affecting presence is an act in the animation of the world, subsequently to be respected for its own sake—as in cultures enacting an aesthetic of beauty—or else for the sake of what it can *do* in the world, as in those cultures enacting an aesthetic of dynamism.

Consciousness determines and vivifies the spatio-temporal existence of the work—its dynamics, its aboutness (or, since it is self-contained, its *is*-ness)—endowing it with the actuality of being. *Consciousness-instilled* is the genius of the affecting presence which transmutes base physical properties into immedia, a melange into a masterpiece. Consciousness, after the elegance and the economy of being, is one and what it inhabits becomes it, just as it becomes what it inhabits, transfiguring it—transfiguring itself—establishing different things in similar ways, through similetic equivalents so that the affecting universe, despite physical differences among the materials of which its works are made, is really one, one embodiment of itself as ultimate medium. In the affecting presence we witness consciousness itself laid bare and existent. So it is that it is *the given* of the affecting presence and so it is that the affecting presence is itself given, an irreducible, whole and self-existent fact in the universe. The affecting presence incarnates consciousness itself, in its own terms, and it arrests flux, fixes the mutable, renders physical the metaphysical.

The simple but very important implication of all this

for the anthropologist is that he has presented to him in the affecting presence the *very consciousness* of a people, the particular conditions under which their human existence is possible. Thus is opened up to him his first prise upon that sole anthropology which can be *humanly* meaningful, the anthropology of experience, the answer to that query the anthropologist has ever held at the back of his mind—*what*, that question asks in insistent childish wonder, *is it like to be somebody else*? He has confounded the answer with the mere collecting of artifacts and data, with assemblages of "information" articulated into structures and of relationships extrapolated into networks, looking ever in the outward for the magical essence which exists only in the inward.

I have described consciousness as an electric engagement with the world such that the world is constituted, basically, in accordance with certain spatio-temporal shapes and processes which are the quintessence of culture. But I have not yet discussed the primary and distinctive activity of consciousness, *intentionality*,[1] which *is* the electricity of engagement. It is the energy of consciousness. Consciousness is invariably consciousness of something, so that without intention consciousness cannot exist. But in the instance of the affecting presence, certain elaborations must be made upon this central characteristic of consciousness. When we witness the affecting presence we fix our con-

---

[1] Because of the orthographic similarity between this word and "intensionality," which is used throughout this work, I shall in subsequent paragraphs use "focus," "engagement," "apprehension," and "directedness" for *intentionality*; and their participial forms (focusing, engaging, directing) for the process form of *intention*, which is *intending*.

sciousness on that which has already been the recipient of its creator's intentional act and indeed incarnates it. It is therefore the case that the witness to the affecting presence directs his consciousness upon distilled consciousness already intended and incarnated. For this reason alone, the apprehension of the affecting presence is an event in consciousness different from all others.

There is not, to paraphrase what I long ago learned as an esoteric truth, any conceivable point or instant in the affecting presence which is not a center of incarnated consciousness, celebrating its own presence. The creator of the work labors to transmute each millimeter, each millisecond of the affecting presence from mere physicality into consciousness-burdened immedia—all to the end of forceful apprehension. He achieves much more than mere focus, it seems, in the arduously achieved charge and drama of focus. This focused and distilled consciousness which he creates had best be called not *intention* but *attention*. So it is that, respecting consciousness in the affecting presence, one had more aptly to speak of *attentionality*. The consciousness focused into the work of affecting presence both perdures and does so with such virtuosity that the terms of consciousness are *celebrated*. After all, if the consciousness incarnated in the affecting presence were not qualitatively different from ordinary consciousness, we should undoubtedly pay little more attention to it than we do to other objects and events which simply locate and focus our consciousness.

Let us look at a work of Goya's in order to examine this phenomenon. For this purpose I have chosen (plate 19) his "Prison Scene," a work suffused with an electricity of attentional engagement . . . with space, with light, and with the presented human condition. The work is dramatic, compelling, and bound to engage not only our sense of the aesthetic—which is to say our interest in the *means* by which the work incarnates feeling—but our sense of the human situation as well, of its dramatic *is-ness*.

To comment on how the work has the shape and process of consciousness requires terms of an analysis not yet made. Therefore, let us take certain positions as given. Let us assume that the Western sensibility is built on a consciousness that is construed of continuity and, simultaneously, of *both* intension and extension. Let us consider space, for example, both the space of a work as well as the space within which a work exists. To do so persuades one immediately that the Western consciousness is comprehensive both of macro- and micro-space, both the ambient space within which the work is held as well as that space of attention which is created within the work. We pay great attention to the context within which a work exists, from the plain wall of neutral color upon which it hangs to the frame which surrounds it, making a space declaration within this larger area. When we consider the "Prison Scene," we see that a dramatized space is a significant portion of its affecting area.

The concern we show for the space pertinent to a work is in marked contrast with the concern of the traditional Yoruba for the object itself in terms of its relationship to a quite specific power. This is, in spatial terms at least, a further instance of Yoruba intensionality, for the only pertinent space of a work—and that, I think, not affectively—is that actually pre-empted by the work. That the Yoruba work exists as an urgent object in a complexly articulated web of urgencies is an additional consideration which may not concern us here.

Through the imperatives of his European consciousness—full-spectrumed and continuous—Goya charges "Prison Scene" with the heavy and dramatic attentionality of his genius, focusing with rich power, through the medium of the particularity of his subject, upon the cultural consciousness which underlies and validates his work. This process in turn so enriches each point upon which the consciousness may be fixed that "Prison Scene" becomes the powerful work it is.

Painting in this and related traditions which present man in pertinent emotionality is possible only because the artist enjoys access to both the greatest and the smallest possible exploitations of space. Irony, for example (with which this painting abounds) seems to me possible only under the circumstance of a consciousness built upon the simultaneous exploitation of both intension and extension. I do not know of irony in any traditional Yoruba work, for example. Satire there is, to be sure, but satire is a matter of allusioning to a referent external to the work. It thus does not involve the spatial (or temporal) existence *of the work*. Irony, in contrast, is a function of the inner conditions of the work. Irony demands range.

In "Prison Scene" we are presented with a full and bitter moment of the world in which the unbearable and degrading suffering of man is thrown into more bitter pain because of the context of light within which it exists. This is possible, to be sure, only because both intension and extension are exploited in the creation of this affecting presence—intension in the pin-pointed

misery of the prisoners, extension in the great doorway
into the day's infinity . . . in the contrast between light
and dark. That this same darkness and light have
allegorical values as well serves to underscore and to
reinforce the presentation of the basic power of the
principle of consciousness which Goya is enacting in the
work. Nor can we ignore the force created by the
enactment of continuity through the agency of the serial
realization of so many stages between bright light and
impenetrable gloom, and equally by the continuity of
the series of bodies which extends from the light into
the darkness.

Attentionality is compounded of several activities,
first among which is selectivity, specificity. If we consider
"Prison Scene" and the Ogun axe, for example, we see
that both works are precise in their presentation. There
is no fuzziness, or clutter, or unintended ambiguity. This
is to be expected for attentionality is a special instance
of focus and therefore it must be consciousness of
something in particular. Of course, those objects and
events for which the consciousness opts in the world
outside the affecting presence—that world which is
sometimes stolen from (its forms transfigured by consciousness indwelling) in order to create the affecting
presence—are likely to be less favorably arrayed and
certainly not in nature in as complementary an ambient
space as are the people in "Prison Scene" or as excitingly
configured and textured as in the Ogun axe. Thus it
is that, while specificity is the characteristic of the
consciousness in attentionality, the thoughtful and vir-
tuoso execution of the work in trenchant and illuminating consciousness is the only way selectivity can be
achieved. We are by pattern selective in our perceptions

of the natural world, of course. But such patterns are our ground, and we are not aware of them; they are our all, the possibility of our whole perceived universe, operating upon an a-structural chaos to impose structure and to achieve focus—with a welter of "noise," objects and events on the periphery of our patterns, or irrelevant ones in the fields of our focus, cluttering our perceptions. But in attentionality in the affecting presence selectivity is made to operate in such a fashion that this is no longer the case. In the affecting presence the field of our perceptions is cleared up; the welter of the natural world is suspended in favor of the order of the uncluttered world of consciousness executed purely and unpretentiously in its own terms. It is in this sense that it is sometimes said of a painting or a sculpture—of an affecting work—that it presents an "ideal" world, though of course sometimes this ascription is made to the aboutness of the work if it depicts some pleasant and unlikely arcadia.

Attentionality is characterized also by fixity. In contrast to the world of protean variability and miscellaneity given to the probing consciousness where time and flux are of the essence of man's own restless drive to fix meaningfulness upon all, in contrast to this the world consciousness creates in the affecting presence, in celebration of itself, abides. Consciousness persists changeless within the viable structures of the works of affecting presence. In fixity it perceives itself in repose and, what is more, it recognizes a truth about itself, which is to say that it validates as accurate and authentic the presented incarnation of its own being. It is this fact which, for the individual co-cultural with a work, provides the basis for a *possible* criticism, one based upon the work's *adequacy in and of consciousness.* In a culture in which types and rules and tradition are important, as among the Yoruba, one overwhelmingly encounters in the affecting presence the fixity of consciousness rather than the richness seen in its adaptability to the needs of individual genius. The work of contemporary artists, deviating from these normative forms into the individualism of diverse and particular aboutnesses, represents a profound change in this respect. Traditional Yoruba forms have presented the immutability of consciousness. This is not to espouse the exploded notion of the "anonymity" of the artist, but rather to speak to the overwhelming importance of classes of works. In a culture in which greatest value is placed on individuation and on the personality of the artist, on the other hand, the situation is the opposite. Here one stands face to face with the consciousness not only of man, let us say of Western man, but of a still living Beethoven and Shakespeare, whose consciousness is yet incarnated in the act of being in which it endured centuries ago during the extended present of the work's creation. In either case, the arrest of flux thus situates the affecting presence in an eternal, affecting present.

Engagement is the third characteristic of attentionality, and is to be identified as that quality operating simultaneously with selectivity and fixity which endows the work with manifest life. Engagement is the lodestar of focus for the work's aboutness—its is-ness—its attentive center of gravity, its existential central nervous system. The engagement in "Prison Scene" exists in the sense of imprisonment developed by the contrast between inside and outside, and asserted chiefly by the series of diminishing elliptical and circular forms—from the vast one of the outside, to the dimmer one of the arch, to its terrible diminution in the iron circle holding the chain which restrains the supine prisoner. Misery and restraint constitute the powerful affecting, kinaesthetic engagement of the work. The most compelling engagement of the Ogun axe is the imperative to assert the most radical and atomistic frontal continuity.

Finally, attentionality is characterized by tension, which is the product of the assertion in immediate and most intimate contiguity of all these previous characteristics. This is possible owing to the fact that these features are not discrete but rather are only discernible points along a continuum. Tension is the electric by-product of their co-existence, honing to an edge, swelling with verve. It is the saturation of the work with consciousness focused fine and true, bringing about the absolute transfiguration of the totality of the work from physical properties into an eventuation of immedia into an affecting presence.

The affecting presence is a work in consciousness, it is not a device which symbolizes consciousness. It is on the contrary an enactment of attentionality perpetrating a particular work not only in its specificity but also in terms of those basic conditions, existing antecedent to and irrespective of any explicit conceptions concerning it, which establish a style of consciousness characteristic of the culture. The affecting presence exists by virtue of its relationship with consciousness, namely that it incarnates consciousness and does not merely reflect the fact that it is a result of conscious activity—as a mere artifact might. But so does a computer incorporate consciousness, as well as does a textbook. But the consciousness incorporated in a computer is hidden; it is a mere internalized process which is not exposed to a witness so that its very enactment of itself might enchant him. As for a textbook, it enacts indeed, but only data and the methods of argument and instruction. It is only the affecting presence which both discloses the fullness of its establishment in consciousness and does so for the purposes of exploiting the aconceptual, averbal dimensions of our being and in such a way that the feelings become essentially involved. The affecting presence finds a significant part of its special nature in the fact that it *celebrates* consciousness, in consciousness' own terms, rather than merely analyzes its selected objects and events in the thin stratum of reason.

I have tried to show this celebrative nature of the affecting presence with respect to its most general dimensions—the cultural mode of the consciousness in which it exists. Further I have done so not only because I am interested in the affecting presence, but also because I am interested in the generalization we call *culture* and wish to see how it is that the former repeats the conditions of the latter.

PART TWO

THE WELLSPRING OF CULTURE

4

Myth and Mythoform

We have paid attention to how a work in affecting
presence is presentational, but we have not given consideration to the reason why it is affecting, and surely this
is its critical second dimension. If we say of the affecting
presence only that it celebrates consciousness, we say
what it does but fail to reveal why this act of celebration
should be imbued with affect. Let us leave aside any
consideration of a work's specific attentionality, such
as that it may be a carving of an ancestor, and consider
instead its general cultural properties—atomistic intensive continuity in the works of the Yoruba, for instance.
We have seen that these disciplines are enacted in
sculpture, in painting, and in narrative. These same
disciplines are to be found constituting dance and music
as well—as I have demonstrated in *The Affecting Presence*. Indeed there I also suggested clues to the perception of these disciplines at work in other areas of Yoruba
life. In other words, what I have identified as the
conditions of being in the affecting presence are to be
found throughout the culture. This is not surprising,
given the tendency toward economy in man's behavior—
as a state which argues against chaos—and the resultant
patterning and integration of the lives of himself and
his peers into culture.

For at irreducible minimum, culture is a viable pattern in the consciousness, a structure and a dynamic of engagement, a "code" of awareness that instills each person, causing him to inherit and in turn to help constitute his culture, dictating the terms under which the world is to be perceived and experienced ... made *actual*. Whether this cultural "genetic" code is turned in viability upon one segment of the spectrum of experience or another is not a factor of significant difference. Thus all of visible culture may be viewed as a projection of this pattern in consciousness. It is perhaps easier to apprehend aspects of this pattern in the affecting presence owing to the fact that it is a direct and presentational celebration of this very patterning itself.

It is clear therefore that at the cultural level the affect of the affecting presence derives from the fact that what are celebrated are the conditions of consciousness. The affecting presence is an act of cultural compulsion, one which enables the human consciousness to validate and to regenerate itself through celebrative auto-presentation. The widespread association of affecting works with religion is rather to be expected than remarked. For "the god" does indeed exist in the affecting presence, if for the moment we regard the god to be the ultimate expression by projection of those principles of the establishment of consciousness which make human life possible. The work of affecting presence is affecting because it enacts in a special way, namely by presentation and celebration, the existential and generative germ of the culture. This is why the affecting presence in all cultures is sometimes venerated, sometimes credited with the power to work good or evil, and is nearly universally valued greatly and accorded distinctive treatment.

The terms of the existence of a culture cannot be celebrated in any condition other than that of affect. Such terms exist only and ever in a state of value. They are the deepest order of man's vision of reality. Their presence humanizes him; they are as basic to his existence and as little subject to his intellectual awareness as his blood pressure. They are the unattended hum of the generation of his human being.

There is then this cultural principle which, nervating, spreads from its base throughout our human being. To explain this principle I postulate the existence of a cultural myth which is without specific content but which has a particularity of form and process. I suggest that we learn this myth with awesome aptitude and hungry avidity in our earliest life and that it patterns all subsequent encounters into *experience.* Further, this myth is only grossly amenable to conceptualization for the simple reason that it is not itself conceptual, lying anterior to the processes of the reason. I postulate that one cannot study this myth solely through language, as some of us have been wont to do, because it is no more inherent in language than it is in religion, that it is as fundamental to social organization as it is to vision, and that it is to be seen best in *all* of culture. The primordial condition of this myth is as anterior to feeling as it is to concept, though it must enact itself in these domains. It is *ground*—preconcept, prefeeling, prebelief—*ground* pure and simple. It exists as a deep reality which, of itself, lies forever hidden, and its sole "language" is the totality of our existence. And all this is not only as it must be but also as it should be, for this living myth is as rich as it is, perhaps, in direct relation to the extent that it is reclusive and esoteric.

This deep cultural myth I postulate I shall call the *mythoform* (though I shall often shorten the form to *myth*, simplicitur). The mythoform is strong, viable, subtle, inescapable, pervasive—operating behind each possibility of man's relationship with the world, refracting through each sense and each faculty into terms appropriate to them.

Only the mythoform can satisfactorily answer those questions about culture which have for so long bedevilled us—how to account for the concordance of the arts, the symmetry of change, the rationale of syncretization, the selectivity of acculturation . . . the homogeny of culture. It is the mythoform which—once postulated, examined, and entertained—can constitute that point of departure from which becomes possible an anthropology of experience—a truly humanistic anthropology—taking as its starting point the *being* of the individual, and fanning out from this interiority to that lived order of the perceived world which is his formulable culture. This is precisely the opposite approach to the traditional anthropological one which both begins and ends in the observable world—that world the anthropologist can through inquiry and response structure into what he believes to bear reasonably close relationships to the lived reality of the world of the people he studies. Such anthropologically described worlds have little expectation to penetrate that lived uniqueness in which other peoples' lives are lived.

The mythoform is the pure principle of cultural being and so lies as anterior to time and space as it does to both concept and feeling. Nonetheless it must live, by which I mean enact itself, in these ways of living the world, exploiting the possibilities of continuity and discontinuity, of intension and extension. It is because these variables of time and space are so discrete and so observable that the affecting presence affords an excellent opportunity for the study of the mythoform. Indeed it is not accidental that it is through my work with the affecting presence that I am led to this present writing. Indeed it is inevitable since the affecting presence bears a special relationship to the mythoform and to those filial myths of the senses and the faculties which it sires as it refracts through their prisms shining out upon the world, lighting our way to engagement with it. This special relationship derives from the fact that when confrontation occurs between the mythoform and the materials of volume, time, color, etc. of which the work is made it is *immediate*, with the former pre-empting the latter in such a way that it incarnates itself according to its own ineluctable nature. Thus if one adequately studies the affecting presence, the apprehension of some of the contours of the mighty mythoform is inevitable.

Further, the affecting presence not only incarnates, it also celebrates the mythoform, by which I mean that it not only assents to its role as incarnator but that it also does so for the very fact of this assenting. Celebration is the unique and definitive function of the affecting presence. Because the affecting presence, a subject, is a celebrative presence, it enjoys a special vitality—the ego-vitality indeed that one expects of a subject. Such a work is both affecting and a presence, it is clear, owing to the fact that it incarnates the mythoform. The basis of our being, our human principle, cannot be *presented* to us as a pauper, it must come burdened with its attendant richnesses of affect. And since it is the principle of our human life, its presentation can only be in terms of that quintessential and ineradicable life that is its necessary condition of being. What is presented in the affecting presence, I think, is revered in religion as well, though in disguised fashion since, given its secrecy and its sometimes obscure symbolism, religion rather tends to enigmatize than to present the mythoform.

Because of the special relationship which the affecting presence bears to the mythoform, and because it is the point of our departure into this inquiry into the mythoform itself, we shall be rewarded by a further brief note upon the affecting presence, which is that one must distinguish the work of affecting presence from the work of mere facticity, such as a tool, or a word, or an icon—a cross for instance. For a tool, while undeniably a result of conscious purpose, unlike the affecting presence is not intended to perpetrate consciousness by duplicating its very form and process. It is merely the case that its functional role exists within the world of the consciousness' devising. Nor does a word or a cross *present*, for neither is directly constituted of or celebrative of the root stuff of consciousness itself, having rather to do with the informing intelligence, which is but one highly specialized feature of consciousness, the probing life of the mythoform.

We are to find in the affecting presence the shape of consciousness, the contours of myth, the structure of being. I have already described how the work exists physically, and I have shown how these parameters of time and space operate with identical discipline in various media despite the physical differences among them. I have called these equivalent phenomena *similetic equivalents*. I have also shown that other areas of behavior show similar discipline. Thus, for example, extension in the affecting presence has as its similetic equivalent range of spectrum in other areas of behavior; intension is matched by the inhibition of range, and so on. What spatio-temporal conditions constitute the affecting presence, then, or embody our social behavior are the metaphoric *modus vivendi* of their perpetration of the culture's living myth—*metaphoric* because they are not the myth itself but the flesh of the myth's enactment.

The parameters of myth must be livable, which is to say that they must be enactable ... must have consequence in space and time, interior as well as exterior, and in all probability *both*. The parameters of myth (which is the living synapse between the human self and the world) therefore are to be seen in its consequences, which are definitive, without alternative, and hence obligatory, distinctive, and lived—which is to say real, absolute, cultural and historical, and existential. They are in a word constitutive of the lived world, and that collocation of them which is the myth of a particular people in the *pattern* according to which the lived world is constituted is *the sentence* which in omnipresent utterance causes the world to be. That utterance is achieved by man in his own being, including of course—preeminently—that essence of his own being which he sets free in the world as the affecting presence.

Myth's consequences, with their essential quality of vitality, present actuality. It is for this reason that we cannot say of a work of affecting presence that it is in any fundamental means *virtual*, for quite to the contrary, and perfectly obviously, since it presents the myth, it can only be veritable.

Myth is culture-specific, which is to say that it is

established in a given manner and is of a given constitution definitive of a given culture. It exists in particular contours and tensions which are the form and process of being. In these formal and dynamic terms myth defines the world for those who live within the validating matrix of its inextricable and ineffable cultural world-plasm. Here are established the only possibility of feeling felt, the only option for belief believed. All that people are and all that they do is under the governance of this cultural myth. The mythoform is a living principle. It is our distinctively human, cultural principle. It solely constitutes our being and what more predictable than that we should celebrate it! It is clear that so subtle, so ultimate a ground might be difficult to ascertain, for—save from the vantage point of another culture, another epoch, or the ground of particular gift—it cannot readily be observed. But pattern finders who grant the singular role of the work of affecting presence and who hold their imaginations adroit, in athletic trim, can intuit the profound presence of the mythoform's mighty being more readily than can those who are plagued with imaginal arteriosclerosis.

Given the universal pervasiveness of the mythoform among its people, there can be little wonder that there should be about it an obligatory and wholly believed quality. This profound and esoteric and generative foundation I have chosen to call *myth*. Myth—*this* myth—is the sheer naming of being. In any culture, this myth is quickly and early learned, for without it experience is impossible. Sensation is possible, to be sure, but experience: *no*. In ways we perhaps do not know the new human makes vast inferences, leaping quickly to the apprehension of the cultural myth in the most

miraculous learning leap of his life. With dizzying speed
he learns the enacting formula of his culture, and this
is the touchstone to his being. He exists forever thereafter held as firmly in its sway as he is in gravity's.

When we understand this and when we understand
that the work of affecting presence is a direct presentation of this mythoform, and that the work is in only
one part—and that the most obvious—concerned with
"content," then we begin to apprehend the true being-
fulness of the affecting presence. Now do we perceive
that the great work of affecting presence is not great
only because of its theme but, fundamentally, because
of the virtuosity and amplitude with which it enacts
the absolute and simple being of the myth. For while
in every affecting presence the myth is wholly pervasive,
yet it is only in the work of genius that the creator
of the work realizes his powerful intimacy with "the
universal" and so celebrates the myth, and his intimacy
with it, for its own sake.

Some may regret that I propose yet another meaning
for *myth*. While I can be sympathetic to this position,
yet at the same time I must protest that there is no
other word which will as satisfactorily name this principle I have described. I call this culturally defined and
culture-defining, life-endowing formula for the consciousness *myth* because it is believed; because it is not
held subject to proof, which indeed is irrelevant to it;
and because it is ever seminal, generative—seeding, ger-
minating, growing. Because it has these properties it
has life itself. And because it lies unperceived, explicitly,
it also enjoys the further powers of mystery and magic.
As a matter of fact, *myth* has been evolving toward

the meaning I here assign it. There is little merit in tracing out the historical development of the term from its meaning of *legends about the gods* to its more generalized aspect under which it designates a theme in human activity, a motif which has a profound and esoteric meaning that plays a seminal role in man's life. Myth in this latter sense has been embraced by both art and literary critics, but more notably so in the works of the man who, chiefly, headed in this direction, Carl G. Jung, a brilliant thinker whose innovative insight is incomparably broad and rich, and infinitely subtle. Myth, for Jung, is a structure of the psyche. "Myths," he asserts, "have a vital meaning. Not merely do they represent, they *are* the psychic life."[1] While he makes this observation as pertaining to "the primitive tribe," we have no reason to accept this limitation. It is a human phenomenon he names. "The fact that myths are first and foremost psychic phenomena that reveal the nature of the soul is something (the mythologists) have absolutely refused to see until now." And finally:

> Primitive man's [for which we may read, simply, *man's*] knowledge of nature is essentially the language and outer dress of an unconscious psychic process. *But the very fact that this process is unconscious gives us the reason why man has thought of everything except the psyche in his attempt to explain myths* (my italics). He simply doesn't know that the psyche contains all the images that have ever given rise to myths, and that our unconscious is an acting and suffering subject with an inner dream . . .[2]

[1] C. J. Jung, *Archetypes and the Collective Unconscious*, ed. G. Adler, tr. R. F. Hull, Bollingen Series, Vol. 20 (Princeton: Princeton University press, 1969), p. 154.

[2] Ibid., pp. 6-7.

Jung's great contribution is to remove *myth* from the domain of literary morphologists and give it to the student of human being. Myths are not merely etiological tales. They are rites of being.

Jung sees myths as he sees archetypes, namely as specific structures, with discrete imprints such that they manifest themselves with distinct, nonvariable *generic* content, allowing of course for the inevitable idiosyncratic aspects of individual occurrences which must however be seen *sub specie aeternitatis* lest their often obfuscating vagaries might tend to obscure the underlying basic myths or archetypes.

The view here, in contrast, is that it is not the fact that "a myth" is "a structure" of the psyche, but that *the myth* is *the* structure of the psyche. It is that there is a deeper myth which is the fertility principle of consciousness, bringing it leaping forward into life; that this principle is whole—total—and without discrete content. It is rather a ground which makes both perception and cognition possible. Jung's discrete "mythogems" are but aspects of this basal myth, aspects expressed in verbal terms, torn from what is but one of the bands of incarnation through which the mythoform reveals itself. The unity of our essence must be channeled through the multiple conduits of our perceptions and faculties if human existence in an external world is to occur. It is only at those rare moments of greatest inspiration that inwardly we know that oneness of our interiority which lies beyond word, beyond sight, beyond any sense or any conception, yet which is generative of the general nature of them all.

There is to the consciousness a wholeness which Jung does not specifically conceive and so does he see as myths what are in fact but splinters of the myth. The chief obstacles to his perception of the unified consciousness are his commitment to the multiplicity of archetypes and his conception of an "unconscious." With respect to this latter point, according to the view here, an "unconscious" is inconceivable, as for that matter is a subconscious. The phenomena which are accommodated by these terms had best be seen rather as functions of the memory. What are attributed to the unconscious and the subconscious are in reality but in the reservoir of the consciousness. They are in file in the inactive consciousness.

There can be little doubt that consciousness is overwhelmingly confounded with the verbal. The execution of this preclusive metonymy aborts our knowledge about the whole by leading us to think that the part is all there is. Indeed, this is precisely the reason why myth has for so long a time been identified solely with its splinters in words. Heidegger is aware of this state of affairs, though from a somewhat different perspective and in the service of a slightly different point. "Perhaps ... what we call feeling or mood here and in similar instances is more rational (vernünftiger), that is, more intelligently perceptive (vernehmender), because more open to Being than all reason (Vernunft) ..."[3]

Jung's myths are related to his key concept of archetypes, which are the factors of the psychic life that, obscurely, are presented in myths. But no matter what high reward many of Jung's ideas hold for the anthropologist, at least one aspect of the formulation of the idea of the archetypes must always present considerable difficulty, namely, the notion of "universality"[4] which

[3] Albert Hofstadler, Richard Kuhn, eds., *Philosophies of Art and Beauty: Selected Readings in Aesthetics from Plato to Heidegger* (New York: Modern Library, Inc., 1964), p. 656.

[4] Jung, *op. cit.*, pp. 44-45.

has been ascribed to the archetype. Jung suggests that archetypes are the unconscious images of instincts;[5] thus would their universality follow. He further asserts their universality in the following: "In view of the fact that all affirmations (such as rebirth) relating to the sphere of the suprasensual are, in the last analysis, invariably determined by archetypes, it is not surprising that a concurrence of affirmations concerning rebirth can be found among the most widely different peoples."[6] But one must recall that Jung was writing at a time when Levy-Bruhl was an undisputed Titan; when the "collective representation" was accepted in psychology and sociology; when the "contemporary ancestor" view of "the primitive," (who was very much a collective person), prevailed in anthropology; and when the motif approach dominated the study of the "folk tale."

It follows from this that Jung's approach to the psyche is subject to the same suggestiveness and to the same limitations as those well-known views of his comtemporaries. For example consider that his approach to the psyche is a substantive one—"The archetype is essentially an unconscious *content*"[7] (my italics)—and that he specifically likens to the motif approach the study of mythology. Thus is his study subject to the same strictures: the archetype like the motif, is perhaps an adequate *inventorying* concept, but it is not a useful *explanatory* or analytic one since it ignores considerations of context and function.

Let us consider an example—not from narrative but from painting—a motif, nonetheless . . . an archetype, to be sure: that theme Jung calls the one of the "dual

[5] Ibid., p. 44.
[6] Ibid., p. 116.
[7] Ibid., p. 5.

mothers."[8] He considers Leonardo's painting, "St. Anne, The Virgin, and the Christ Child" in terms of Freud's interpretation—namely that in painting two mothers Leonardo was in effect enacting a circumstance of his own life, for he is reputed to have had two mothers. Freud thus interprets the painting as "caused" by Leonardo's personal unconscious. But Jung rejects this—gently chiding Freud for seeming not to know that St. Anne was the Virgin's mother. Further, Jung asks how to explain, in fundamental terms, the numerous other painters of the same subject who in fact had only one mother. He concludes that if the painting represents the theme of dual mothers it does so not at the level of the personal but rather of the collective unconscious, thus accounting for the similar works of a host of other painters.

But one may reasonably inquire whether the dual mother (loving and terrible) does not in her antithetical terms, which cause her to encompass opposites, assert something of what appears to be an inherent feature of Western dialectical thought—namely, oppositionality. One is further prompted to inquire whether among the Yoruba, where there is ample reason to believe that the principle of thought is not oppositional and synthetic, the theme of dual mothers would be read in the same fashion rather than either as co-mothers (a sociological fact) or possibly, as successive mothers? Certainly the Yoruba Christian might regard the personages of the da Vinci painting simply as grandmother, mother, and child—a simple, syndetic instance of generations supported by the actual biographical facts of the case.

One can, in short, index the substantive themes of

[8] Ibid., p. 47.

a culture or of the world after a system of archetypes or motifs; but at the end one has only that—an index. He may have no certainty that the themes indexed are comparable in accordance with any criteria other than those of mere content. So it is that to use archetypes as cross-cultural analytical devices is to be without validity. If one cannot use "archetypes" cross-culturally, it follows that this is precisely because they are not universal. I do not mean as classes of events within cultures but as substantive classes carrying cross-cultural validity. Therefore despite what otherwise might be the attraction of such an option the anthropologist must reject the universality of the archetype—even of the archetype of bi-polarity which Levi-Strauss proffers.

This is not to question the validity of Jung's observations on the *archetypes* as descriptive categories of the *content* of the psyches of the inheritors of Western European culture or to deny the possibility of archetypes as substantive classes in other cultures *in those cultures' own terms*. On the other hand, however, neither is this the place in which the Jungian psychology must be defended. We can only say that whatever the validity of the archetypes Jung has described, they cannot be construed as other than Western and therefore not *per se* basic structures of man's mind.

What Jung perceived as archetypes were in fact some substantive items or motifs which recurringly derive from the generative principle of the psyche sired out of the Greco-Roman-Hebraic historical flood. Why these motifs recur one does not know—perhaps because they are particularly potent presentations of the psyche, perhaps because they accrue authority and validation through history. Whatever the case, this was the question which beguiled Jung, this and the fact that these motifs can be found in some form or other in various non-European parts of the world. It may be that they are presentations of some universality, in which case one can argue something in behalf of the psychic unity of mankind. But in any case it is not the image itself which must interest us but the dynamic which lies behind it, creating it. So also is it with respect to the archetypes with which Jung was concerned primarily, namely those of the European consciousness; here too one must properly be concerned not with the archetypes but with that structure and that dynamic that generates them. Although I reject the term for use here, nonetheless one may say that while Jung perceived the archetypes, he did not see *the* archetype which lies beyond them, the basal myth to which they must each in turn trace their genesis and from which they derive their power. Not unlike others, he did not look deeply enough for he was content to see the phenomena of his own culture as universal, despite an impressive experience with and learning in other cultures. In any case, Jung himself sees the archetypes as presented to the psyche in the service of a common end which he identifies as *individuation*. This term itself abounds with mythic connotations for the European. By this I mean to say that individuation is related in a particularly meaningful way to what we shall subsequently see is at least a significant part of the myth of this Western psyche I have been writing of, suggesting as it does the emergence of the new as a result of a dialectic (in his terms) between the consciousness and the unconsciousness.

I am fully aware that in speaking of the "Western" or the "European" psyche I am operating at a level of generalization that will worry some readers. Few are more aware than I that the cultural and epochal spread that must be taken into account in "The Western Psyche" is so great as to be staggering. And yet we have in anthropology spent so much time collecting data that have not led to significant generalizations about man that I have decided in my work to reach those significant generalizations that seem on the basis of wide evidence to be reasonable and then to let the data follow as they may in examination of the hypothesis. Yet, if I chose generalizations merely because they are "reasonable," I would be engaged in little more than a form of intellectual sport. The generalizations I choose to write about are those which seem inevitable and which seem most greatly to explain the nature of man.

In what respect do those myths with which Jung is concerned embody the mythoform, if indeed they do? And, more importantly, if they do embody it, do they do so in any special way such that their distinction from other narratives is justified on other than the most superficial of grounds, namely that they are stories of gods and heroes and that they often have etiological functions? Before this question can be answered, two facts must be faced. In the first place it follows from the position advanced here that all human acts are generated from the mythoform, and in some sense or other, if the acts in question are studied long and imaginatively enough—and indeed if the myth is adequately perceived—the determination of the myth in the action will be ascertained. In the second place we must bear in mind the special nature of the affecting presence with respect to incarnating the very myth itself and to doing so in the myth's own terms.

We must bear in mind that some of the "myths" Jung

is concerned with are merely expository or discursive. They do not become works of affecting presence. The affecting media are not exploited toward the end of realizing the myth as a subject. This is the case, for example, with most of the "myths" which have been recorded for the Yoruba—they are mere expositions of something or other and are usually so simple and of so little interest that they bear no significant (or even slight) relationship to the music, the dance, or the sculpture. What is true of the Yoruba materials is true of the corpus of available materials on other peoples as well. Many available "myths" are simply not affecting works. Such accounts bear only the same relationship to the mythoform that ordinary discourse does, and what that may be it is not our present purpose to inquire.

But there are other works, narratives, which do and are intended to become works of affecting presence. Now the work of affecting presence eventuates by virtue of the fact that in respect of insistent disciplines upon the media and the content of the work the mythoform becomes incarnated—in spatio-temporal dimensions, in plot dynamics, in the exploitation of imagery, in character development ... in all these the myth enacts itself. Good works enact the myth well, great works enact it powerfully, and bad works enact it ill.

Let us consider for a moment the *Theogony* of Hesiod, a work which has the content required by the traditional definition of "myths" and which is, at the same time, an affecting presence. I shall not pretend to make any analysis designed to reveal the mythoform of a small area of Greece in the eighth century B. C. I shall assert only that the work, even given its enormous age, is unquestionably from a European culture. It is incon-

ceivable that it should be African, for example. Thus
I am guided to search for some of the characteristics
which I have associated with the disciplines of the
European mythoform, for want of any other grid and
on a justification for this search rooted in the "European" quality of the work. Briefly, the work amounts to
a genealogy of the gods, and it is executed in rich
hexameters which are subject to the most careful auc-
torial control. Because *Theogony* is a genealogy,albeit
of a highly complex sort, it achieves a strong continuity,
as indeed it does also from the uniformity of the verse
form. In adhering rigorously to its theme of the origins
of the gods it is intensive, as it is also in the invariability
of its major metrical features. At the same time it is
extensive as well in the richness of imagery in which
it is enacted.

But there are other "myths" more powerful than the
Theogony . . . the Oedipus, for example. I am not thinking
of one of the great literary texts at the moment; instead
I am concerned solely with the situation in which a
malformed man, of dire antecedence, saves his people
and yet condemns himself to an undeserved fate. If for
"malformed" we say merely "extraordinary" and for
"dire" "dread" we reach terms which at a structural
level remind us of the myth of Christ. The great power
of both of these myths, I maintain, derives from the
fact that they perpetrate a most important and rare
kind of incarnation, namely both personify the mythoform itself so that the terms of the myth become actors
in the works. These "myths" thus not only enact the
mythoform in ways already noted as characteristic of
the affecting presence; they *doubly* present it through
the additional dimension of personification. In a "myth"

like Oedipus the cultural and the particular are so merged as to become inseparable, so merged that for the time of a civilization the mind of Western man has been held captive by this profoundly compelling tale, presenting us with an audacious enactment of the principle of our being. Freud came near to seeing this. He recognized the sheer and incredible power of the mere story which, as we know, he understood to be an enactment of certain kinds of family relationships. What he failed to see is that these relationships are themselves enactments of a cultural consciousness. Such works might, conceivably, be called "myths" for an especially trenchant and defensible reason. A second class of stories, like the *Theogony* are to be seen merely as narrative works of affecting presence, while works of the lowest order—those simple expositions about the gods, the creation of the world and of institutions, and about heroes—are not affecting works at all.

It will be rewarding to explore the Oedipus further, but before we can do so it is necessary to search for some of the contours of our own consciousness. In one general term, namely that of its spatio-temporal features, Western European consciousness has stressed the roundedness and the continuity of the experienced world. This explains the predominating tendency of European artists to achieve works as specific eventuations of space and time within the context of a larger and encompassing space or time which the specific concentration of the work is not but which, by contexting that concentration, helps to define it. Paintings typically include a carefully painted context in which the figures, objects, or events which are enacted occur— the space of their occurrence. It is within this space that they extend or intend, as the case may be, in order that their existence in a context might be fully achieved. A ballet occurs within a clearly defined and carefully executed space. Similarly a musical work, executed within the time of our own witnessing of it, swells to fullness or diminishes to a smallness of spectrum, or it speeds or slows within the context of the objective time of our hearing of it. Whatever the artform involved, the point is that it exists contexted so that it may inflex or outflex as the necessity may be in order that it might most believably exist in the world of its making and of our acceptance. Among the Yoruba, in contrast, a work occurs not so much in an "art" time-space as in a social and historical one. "Yoruba" is the context of every Yoruba work in contrast to the entailed visual or auditory or kinetic space-time that is the context of European works. The objective of the European work of affecting presence is the achievement of the particular in the most singular terms possible so that its particularity is for all times established. Thus is the goal of Western art a kind of *truth*—artistic or poetic truth, we are accustomed to call it. Truth is won, in our culture, not through revelation but through dialectic; and truth is a cultural good for us. So the Western work of art both is and enacts a process in dialectic. And as truth is evolutionary so is art, and so are we driven ever in the direction of the synthesis, the ultimate resolution to our artistic problem. So do works succeed works and schools succeed schools. It is possible—as now—that our movement may be in the direction of the new for its own sake. In any case, as we go further, we also go faster, and so the dialectical processes decree that our works in affecting presence become speciated with ever increasing rapidity.

This total exploitation of the spatio-temporal spectrum necessarily implies the incorporation—indeed the embrace (passionate to the Romanticist, decorous to the Classicist) of the extremities, that is to say of both intension and extension. By so combining opposites, Western man says, the real world is made; and in terms of opposites is its true and individuated uniqueness to be perceived. Oppositionality, it follows, is celebrated in the affecting works, presented in terms of a dialectic of polarities—the subject in its space, the particular in the general, the fugue between what is and what is not. Cases in point are the musical conventions of point and counterpoint where separate though complementary tonal points argue in the absence of one another, which is simply to say that point occurs in the absence of the beat of counterpoint, and counterpoint similarly in the absence of point; in the constant search for contrasts in the fugue; in the sonata form with its theme and countertheme; in mirror composition—and indeed even in language about music; the *argument* of a theme, its *resolution*, and in the very name *antiphony*. In painting the impressionists afford an example, for in their works is established a dialectic between permanence and ephemerality, durability and change, the enduring and the instantaneous. In dance the argument is between the body and gravity, and between the dancer's corporeality, which is instrument, and his person, which is poet of his culture's poetic myth. In sculpture stone and steel compete with nothingness for spaces they would not normally pre-empt, as is the case as well in architecture. There are those arts which compete with gravity, those that compete with emptiness, and those that compete with silence.

But is it only the affecting presence we so perceive?

Surely this cannot be the case, for if it is true that the affecting presence is the presentation through enactment of that myth which is the root principle of our consciousness, and if it is true that the myth at this level is prismed into all subsequent visas to the world, then it follows that we must perceive it elsewhere as well, not only *present* in its own terms in the affecting present as *living polarities*, since that is after the nature of the affecting work, but influencing—indeed determining—the structures and functions of other pursuits as well.

Dualities abound, constituting our civilization. Our religion is premised upon good and evil, and indeed could not exist were it not for the presence of evil which endows it with meaning and efficacy. We analyze the unitive work of art into form and content; and we construct a logic based upon right and wrong. Our languages are of subject and object, or of subject and attributes asserted of it—of the permanent to which the transient is fleetingly ascribed: in "John is happy," John endures while the ascription of his happiness in all likelihood is destined to be brief indeed. We could as easily, perhaps, have invented a language in which "John-happying," an assertion which does not pose such contrarieties, conceives of John in the estate of being happy as all there is to be said, and that John-being-happy is only present reality of John. Our science is one of the probable versus the improbable, the workable as opposed to the unworkable, matter and anti-matter—all perhaps, as Conant suggests somewhere, revealing more of the nature of the scientist's mind than of the actual nature of the physical universe. We see the world as delicately constituted of both terms in an infinite system of

contrasting pairs, and bound together by the tension
that exists between them. To be sure one term in each
case is, by definition, of greater value than its opposite.
Needless to say our normative culture pushes us relent-
lessly in the pursuit of the "positive," ever admonishing
us to eschew the "negative"—to pursue science, not
non-science; good, not evil; order, not chaos; the enduring, not the fleeting. In pursuit of the positive terms
our great institutionalized systems are constituted. In
large measure, then, the myth of the consciousness of
Western Europe is the myth of bi-polar oppositions.

In the final analysis, the extent to which the tension
between polarities reflects the only order of the universe
awaits the advent of a new science, a possibility which
need not strike us as outrageous since old sciences have
yielded, giving place to the new, lest one good science
should corrupt and misconstrue the world.

I cannot however judge concerning science and its
polarities. But the pervasion of this same principle of
polarity in the form of various dualisms upon all other
areas of our world and experience is, however, clearly
a function of our myth. It is not in the inevitable nature
of things that there should be two houses of parliament
or of congress; that there should be two effective arms
of government in the United States, one enacting and
one executing, constituting one polarity, with the Supreme Court counterpointing a polarity to both of these
by determining the validity or invalidity of the actions
of the other two. It is not inevitable that the godhead
should reflect the same dualistic model for triad, namely
a polarity, subsequently counterposed by the third
term—as there are two wholly spiritual parts, one formal
and one efficacious, opposed by one corporeal part,

wholly mediative. Finally, it is not inevitable that there should inexorably be a division of the world into friend and foe with the result that the history of our foreign policy in recent years at least is more accurately to be characterized in terms of our determination to identify and to perpetuate enemies than to create friends.

Let us return to "myths" as narratives in order to perceive there enacted this very myth of polarity I have in hypothesis identified as the Western European mythoform. As a first step we must invoke the discipline of continuity, for it plays an especially important role in the enactment of polarity, since it is characteristic of most European narrative that is transmuted into affecting presence that the dialectical process is continuous. This is to say that in the story development *a* is opposed to *b*, producing—in some sense—*ab* which in turn is opposed by *-ab*, yielding *c*—and so on. In order to name this phenomenon (which, the reader may wish to note, is notably uncharacteristic of *The Palm-Wine Drinkard*) of progressive and continuing organic synthesis, we may speak of *polar continuity*.

Further, narrative myths of Western Europe involve the *me* and the *not-me*, or more precisely perhaps, the hero and the not-hero. It is true, of course, that any narrative generates dramatic action by means of opposing characters or forces. This after all is in the nature of story—actors are the means of the enactment of the narrative—and we cannot therefore read the existence of conflict between a hero and an anti-hero necessarily and only as evidence of polar continuity. Or rather, granting that such conflict does present polarity, we are in no position to assert of this situation that it is, being characteristic of the genre, cultural. It is rather that, given the viable mythoform of polar continuity, the sense of conflict is in Western Europe likely to be more developed, of greater elaboration than in other cases—as we may witness in the case of the Yoruba—precisely because its inevitability dictates that it usurp chief interest in and for itself. Further, in the narrative myth of polar continuity, even when such elaboration is not markedly the case, the chief interest of the co-cultural witness to the myth will be centered on conflict. It is in these respects, then, that in part the narrative embodies the mythoform.

Although a bewildering array of kinds of tales has been called "myths," we have agreed here that myths are those tales which in their fictive substance—and not in their structures and dynamics alone—enact the mythoform. Myths, therefore, at least at some point in their lives, excite and enhance belief—or, perhaps more exactly, profound affecting suasion—because through personification they enact the mythoform for the purpose of the cultural edification the witness derives from the rite of beholding immediately and in a special way participating in the celebration of the germinal principle of his human being. It is a situation directly analogous to the belief we feel in witness of any other affecting presence, and of course it is for the same reason, the equivalent or similetic incarnation and enactment of some significant feature (against the background of all the rest of the features) of the myth that founds the consciousness.

The myth of Oedipus has so profoundly incarnated and personified this dialectical aspect of the structure and the process of the European mythoform that, though born in a time more ancient than we can fathom when we encounter it, it yet forces us to reckon with its power. Indeed, in this age so dedicated to analysis of everything conceivable, especially of man himself, it has it seems become a prime myth of our day. It is in any case one of the very few actual myths whose content we seem in some sense to believe. It is therefore a living myth. Levi-Strauss, commenting on the Oedipus myth, interestingly observed that Freud's reconstitution of the Oedipus myth must be counted as one of its incarnations, incarnations which taken all together constitute the entirety of the myth, its *la langue*. Thus does he testify to that continuing vitality which marks its validity.

The mythoformal reading of the Oedipus yields a simpler product than Freud's psychoanalytic one. It is, most basically, a presentation in polar continuity, involving in serial plan, cataclysmic oppositions among successive pairs of polar actors. Its particular significance, to be sure, derives from the overriding bonds of value which should have held these oppositions in dynamic stasis for oppositions are good, and they are necessary to social, ethical, and empirical progress. But some oppositions pervert this good—all the more horrible when, unbeknown to one, what he conceives to be good is in fact evil. What all the expectations of man have proved to be enduring, ennobling, humanizing, proves instead to be the opposite.

The simple though consummately tyrannical order of the universe embodies in its infinity the ultimate writing of reality. But this cold, universal reality, the polar nature of all things, would appear to have been suspended in the case of man, who by integrating the oppositions of his parents is the ultimate synthesis. Yet as Freud saw, this synthesis is more apparent than real. It is a beguiling illusion, and the individual consciousness must define itself in the only way it can, which is to say in opposition to all others. This is the myth of consciousness which enacts itself in the Oedipus. A horrible incest has produced, in dreadful synthesis, the Sphinx, offspring of the Echidna and her own offspring, Orthus, the dog.[9] The deformity which is the Sphinx, issuing from this heinous union, expresses nonetheless the integration of his dam and sire. Mankind can be safe only if the Sphinx is destroyed, and Oedipus, who because of his own deformity (of the foot) is in this small sense analogous to the Sphinx, hence is ritually appropriate for this task in behalf of mankind. His awareness of his own crippledness, whether it makes him especially apt to answer the Sphinx's fatal riddle or not, is—we assume—at least not irrelevant to the puzzle about man based only upon the nature of man's pedality.

Oedipus can slay the Sphinx because, having resolved the paradox of its riddle, he has rendered it powerless; and so he must go the rest of the way in unravelling of this monstrosity of integration by also engaging in precisely the same kind of union which produced the Sphinx. Thus, he marries his own mother and begets not a monster but two sons and two daughters. Through the inevitable sacrifice of himself and his kind, he analyzes the causes of his being once again into their identities of whole and un-monstrous selfness, and mankind is again safe. Once the seed of incest that bore

---

[9] Hesiod, *Theogony*, lines 326-27 (*Hesiod: The Homeric Hymns and Homerica*, Loeb Classical Library, tr. Hugh Evelyn-White [London, Heinemann, Cambridge, Mass.: Harvard University Press, 1936]).

evil has spent itself—perpetrated by gods and destroyed by a hero—Thebes is purged and mankind is released to its natural destiny of utter selfhood. Oedipus is a tragedy of synthesis gone awry.

The gravity of the act which the tragic hero performs in behalf of man is directly measured by the degree to which his story moved the poets of his race and their audiences. The fact that one of the greatest poets of Greece turned his maturest art upon the myth of Oedipus is testimony to the fact that it was deemed worthy, which is to say both profound and noble. We must assume that in writing the Oedipus the poets of Greece were enacting a most luminous, moving, and meaningful theme—the consciousness of the Greeks come to harm. The Greeks are redeemed by a hero who vanquishes the great evil that threatens them, and as his reward he is made to suffer most awfully. Because the parameters of consciousness were perhaps sharper then, the myth was doubtless even more powerful to the Greeks than it is to us who witness it today through eyes of a consciousness more calloused, or more ramified ... or differently ... more diffuse, certainly. We today see the Oedipus not under the aegis of the salvation of man but rather in terms of his sickness. Oedipus stands now not for man saved, but for man damned by the very circumstances of his existence. Freud, expressing the myth of his own time, fixed not upon the noble achievement of Oedipus' tragedy, but upon the mere mechanism by means of which it was brought about. Oedipus himself, like Freud, sees only his crime. But the preservation of man is precisely that act which makes of Oedipus a "person of high estate," for beyond mere kingship, which is his apparent high estate, the magnitude of his sacrifice ennobles him indeed. The inevitability of Oedipus' fate traced for the Greeks the bare and relentless inevitability of fate—whatever the particular conformation may be—that awaits each man and that he must with unflinching valor enact—his own being, we would say now . . . his own consciousness.

Levi-Strauss himself, with some irony, employs those same polarities of consciousness which he has inherited from the Greeks whose myth he appropriates, vindicating the validity of the myth by virtue of his own enactment of it. He himself, quite as he says of Freud, becomes part of the myth (even, since I am aware of my own ironic situation in this regard, as I here do). Levi-Strauss sets for himself the task of trying to arrange the constituent elements of the Oedipus myth into columns of similar episodes, according to "the principles which serve as a basis for any kind of structural analysis: economy of explanation; unity of solution; and ability to reconstruct the whole from a fragment, as well as further stages from previous ones." Accordingly he derives the following inventory:[10]

These four vertical rows he finds constitute two sets of contrasting pairs, or polarities. The terms of the first pair assert, first (the first column) "overrating of blood relations" while the second column asserts the "underrating of blood relations." The terms of the second set of columns are "the denial of the autochthonous origin of man" and (by virtue of the fact that Oedipus' lameness attests to his identity with chthonian man) "the persistence of the autochthonous origin of man."

[10] Thomas Sebeok, ed., *Myth, A Symposium* (Bloomington: Indiana University Press, 1970), pp. 89-90.

Kadmos seeks his sister Europa ravished by Zeus			
		Kadmos kills the dragon	
	The Spartoi kill each other		
			Labdacos (Laios' father)= *lame* (?)
	Oedipus kills his father Laios		
			Laios (Oedipus' father)= *left-sided* (?)
		Oedipus kills the Sphinx	
Oedipus marries his mother Jocasta	Eteocles kills his brother Polynices		Oedipus = *swollen-foot* (?)
Antigone buries her brother Polynices despite prohibition			

"It follows," he concludes, "that column four is to column three as column one is to column two. The inability to connect two kinds of relationship is overcome (or rather replaced) by the positive statement that contradictory relationships are identical inasmuch as they are both self-contradictory in a similar way."[11]

The mythoformal reading of the Oedipus reveals a drama in contrarieties and syntheses, a horrible synthesis opposed—and resolved—by a splendid hero who, irrespective of the good he had wrought for mankind, must nonetheless suffer. It is a formula familiar in its simplicity. It is moving because it enacts us, attests to and celebrates the conditions of our being. If in its barest terms the myth of Oedipus reminds us further of the myth of Christ (as one of the Trinity, he too bore a *special* relationship to his mother, having in a sense begotten Himself) we will perhaps understand something of the deep mythoformal basis for Christianity's success in Europe.

When earlier I wrote that there is a myth for each form—a form-specific adaptation of the mythoform—I meant that in the domain of the work's spatio-temporal existence there is not only the presence of a typical structure of exploitation so that the work comes to be, but also that there is about that sense of typical structure an oughtness, or imperative, such that variations are violations and are senseless and therefore likely to be rejected. The extent to which in the domain of fictive substance myth also by imperative incarnates into the work is by definition ever approaching totality; this is to say that the shape of consciousness as generative principle pushes aboutness in the direction of the maxi-

[11] Ibid., p. 91.

mal realization of itself. *Oedipus* is "great" because it maximally enacts the mythoform, though it does so with a certain irony. This is why, too, at least some Yoruba find *The Palm-Wine Drinkard* great because it is greatly Yoruba. In the principle of the generation of its aboutness it is ineffably Yoruba.

It is fascinating to inquire whether the Western European polar mythoform exerts any influence upon that explicit ethnoaesthetic which is our own Western aesthetic tradition. I have already mentioned the presence in the Western aesthetic of the distinction between form and content as a basic and characteristic polarity. But other polarities are to be found as well—from the distinction between *imitation* and *imitated* in Plato to that between *world* and *earth* in Heidegger. Further, Western aesthetics have been devoted avowedly to beauty but in fact to "truth." "Euclid alone has looked on beauty bare," Edna St. Vincent Millay writes somewhere, and Keats, as every school child knows, proclaims that "Beauty is truth, truth beauty." Whether beauty or truth is ideal order, or whether virtue is, or "unconcealment," such concepts and not the work itself are of interest to the Western aesthetician. Thus there ever exists, in philosophical speculation, an antiphonal relationship between the work and that which the work discloses—a position to which Langer also is dedicated. We now perceive, ever so much more surely, the extent to which she is *naturally* so directed by the dictates of her cultural consciousness.

What we attempt here is to perceive not only the myth of our own consciousness, but also, in the highest anthropological act (which consists in perceiving the nature of the limitations imposed upon us by our own ethnocentricity, and learning thus what few escapes we can), to perceive something of the nature of other myths radically different from our own. The subsequent objective, quite naturally, is to gain some prise upon the character of the perception of the people co-cultural with a work, to ascertain something of the world of experience of which it is a part, and to comprehend some of the conditions under which it persists in eternal and eloquent being.

The relationship of mythoform to culture is this, that it is the vital, operative principle of culture. Culture, it would follow, is the enactment of this myth writ in its largest possible terms. Of course, it is clear that culture is seldom perceived in the viable terms of its whole and living existence, which is unique, simple, powerful, and infinitely generative. Instead, the large phenomenon of culture is misperceived, apprehended not organically but only through various extrinsic or otherwise not entirely relevant grids—certainly not through grids designed to reveal the myth in its own living reality.

The mythoform is the generative principle of culture and, at the same time (since digging at the root of things we find ourselves anterior to paradox) both the substance of culture and the mode in which that substance is enacted and exists. It is content-less at the same time that it is all content, both actual and conceivable. It is both the ground and the end of all action. There is no object or event of culture that has not been shaped by it; it in turn is shaped by every object and every event. There is no affecting presence whose incarnating spatio-temporal structure and processes and whose intellectible dimensions do not, in irreducible significant base, name its very shape and dynamics.

Culture is the being of myth, and the ideal anthropology is that one which recognizes this fact and bends every effort to the unveiling of the mythoform's informing presence in and beyond the diverse phenomena of the culture, realizing that it is what causes phenomena to be as they are in cultural experience, and in turn using that rich insight in the service of his task, which is to elucidate man.

5

Synthesis and Syndesis

All that I have said of consciousness and of its substratum of myth reveals that the processes of Western European consciousness eventuate in the constitution of reality through analysis and subsequent synthesis; while the Yoruba process of the constitution of reality proceeds through syndetism. These readings appear to be justified by virtue of the wide spectrum exploited in, for example, contemporary Western European presentionality, fully developed even to both extremities of the intensive/extensive continuum, and equally as fully continuous.

The Yoruba syndetic process of abutting apposites presents itself not only in the work of affecting presence. Since it is the name of the Yoruba myth, or of one aspect of it at least, it is accordingly to be seen everywhere. But before we proceed to search for evidences of it elsewhere in Yoruba culture, it will be well to reemphasize several points. First, we must say again of this myth that it is a construct, factored out of the universe of the affecting presence and taken as hypothesis to be the elegant and economical generative principle—the mythoform—that will be seen to order wide and diverse orders of phenomena. Second, we must bear in mind that this is a hypothesis concerning only the

Yoruba. It does not pertain to any other people, whether they be adjacent or distant, or whether they in their own presentational forms also enact intensive continuity. Other peoples, neighboring or far away, may have forms of behavior which appear to be similar, yet we have learned that homologous forms do not necessarily imply identity of significance or function.

In traditional Yoruba culture one is born into a family comprised of a father, his wives, and his wives' children. The physical household consists of quarters for one's father and reasonably identical quarters for the wives, each of whom, together with her children, makes her portion of the family life. A man's marital life thus may be viewed as consisting of so many wiving episodes, each separately enacted at a particular point in his life. From the wife's point of view, upon marriage she becomes but one of several women fulfilling identical roles—a co-wife. All these relationships taken together constitute marriage.

Children are highly prized. They are the spectrumization into the future of a man and each of his wives—and of their ancestors. The operation of the process of reincarnation inhibits the range of greatly differentiated humans who may be born into the family, thus inducing the rule of apposition into the progeny. The soul of a grandparent or a great grandparent stands a strong chance of being born into the successive children of the family. Children whose antecedent souls are recognized are typically named in honor of that reincarnated soul. Thus one encounters very frequently names ending in *-tunde*, thus *Babatunde* meaning that a directly antecedent male has been reincarnated. The family's energies gain strength through such channelling which derives from the inhibition of lineal and generational variation, and they retain their primeness of power. Souls are recycled, with each soul being promised another lifetime of earthly existence when, after the death of its mortal vehicle, it has returned once more to one of the spiritual realms (*orun*). One should note that existence is conceived of as a continuum with the more complex spiritual world being composed of several (an informant has told me six) realms or "heavens," and the mortal world being represented by but one which, however, leads directly back once more into the spiritual dimensions of the continuum of existence. It is Olorun himself, the highest god, who makes these life assignments, and if the body which one is given dies prematurely the spirit is, in some accounts, immediately given another body while in other accounts, it is forced to become a ghost until such time as his normal span shall have been concluded.

Children may be viewed as units or stages in the fluctuation of energy, with the first child being the most important (the most powerful), save for twins, which are markedly more common in Yorubaland than they are elsewhere in the world. A soul is to be conceived of as having both an earthly and a heavenly aspect. It is the former which is born time after time while the heavenly aspect remains, an archetype, in the spiritual realms—except in the instance of twins in which case this archetypal spirit is itself born into one of the bodies. Twins are thus, syndetically, but dual instances of the same force. The two successive children after twins derive names determined by their proximity to twins, so that they are to be viewed as variant aspects of the process of twinning, attenuating through the first after twins and the second after twins to normal child-bearing.

Once again the force of recurring elements is in the direction of appositional continuity.

There is another aspect of the phenomenon of appositional syndetism to be served in the intensive continuum of childbearing: the *abiku*, which there is some reason to believe is related to twins.[1] The abiku are children who are successively born to the same mother only to die, time after time, preferring the spirit world to the human. The abiku and twins both are to be seen as syndetic and appositional variations upon the theme of one soul. So do they permit, even in their "deviance" from the phenomenon of single childbearing, a closely patterned and rigorously inhibited phenomenon of variation. Finally, it is significant to note that souls do not unite to produce new souls. The same ones ever reappear.

The traditional Yoruba grows up under such implicit familial values then as serve to enact the myth. But since in a reasonably homogeneous culture the myth is able straightforwardly and monolithically to inform the range of one's living, the Yoruba enact the myth in other ways as well. The pantheon, for instance, is so finely denominated (there are said to be 401 gods) that it is perhaps difficult to argue appositionality—save in respect of the factor of divinity itself—though of course it is hardly difficult to argue syndetism! The point here, as elsewhere, is that we are presented with a range of phenomena which we attempt, after our hypothesis, to perceive under the auspices of the myth.

At its very base Yoruba religion implies the myth. Christianity is founded upon the notion of alienation between God and man, original sin having established

[1] Marilyn Hammersley Houlberg, "Ibeji Images of the Yoruba," p. 23, pp. 20-27, *African Arts* Vol. VII, No. 1, Autumn, 1973.

a polarity between them. The Yoruba on the other hand
believes that man's natural estate is to be at one with
the positive forces of the universe, forces from which
he is occasionally alienated by means of neglect, error,
or the countervailing energies of witchcraft. For the
Christian, God exists wholly independent of man and
he is opposed by a god of evil; for the Yoruba the gods
and the ancestors have an entirely different relationship
with man, for they are dependent upon him even as
man is dependent upon them. Spiritual and human
forces, in a word, bear additive relationships one to the
other. This is a kind of complementarity and it is defined
in terms of the idea of increase—man feeds the gods,
the gods in turn see to it that man prospers as well.

Yoruba religion is complicated, and it cannot be
treated systematically here. I shall, however, call attention to two of the chief Yoruba gods, Eshu and Ifa.
About Eshu I shall say only that he is the gods'
messenger and the driving trickster and enforcer. He
deceives men, he takes advantage of them, he causes
accidents to befall them. He also punishes them if they
do not fulfill their obligations of sacrifice to the gods.
Eshu delivers sacrifices directly to Olorun, and he is
closely associated with the work of Ifa. But the aspect
of Eshu which is of greatest interest here is that he
is characterized by self-multiplication—infinitely.[2] Since
Eshu is sometimes thought of as the "uncertainty principle," one sees that the infinite multiplication of Eshu
makes all uncertainties subsumable under the aegis of

[2] Robert G. Armstrong. From an unpublished paper "Helping Afri-
cans to Speak for Themselves: The Role of Linguistics." Delivered
before the ixth International Congress of Anthropological and Ethno-
logical Sciences, Chicago, 1973.

one class. Thus is inhibition induced in the ranges of misfortune and thus, also, are intension and apposition introduced into what would otherwise be the chaos of unpredictabilities.

But of course the Yoruba world is predictable. This is precisely the function of Ifa, and it is a nice additive pairing that Eshu (uncertainty) and Ifa (certainty) should be paired in Yoruba religion. They do not become opposites, and enemies. On the contrary they are colleagues in man's fate. They represent the two points of a continuum, and as earthly existence leads back to the spiritual realms, so are certainty and uncertainty more closely related than one might think upon first consideration. Indeed uncertainty is only a certain view of certainty. It is before Ifa.

"Ifa is a system of divination based upon sixteen basic and 256 derivative figures (odu) obtained either by the manipulation of sixteen palm nuts (ikin), or by the toss of a chain (opele) of eight half seed shells."[3] It is a system presided over by Ifa (Orunmila), the god within whose province the system falls. The system of divination itself is premised upon the assumption that all things are known to Olorun, the almighty. But the will of Olorun is never directly knowable by men. It must be revealed by Ifa.

Slightly different procedures are employed for casting the divination depending upon whether the diviner (babalawo) uses loose nuts or the chain. For our present purposes, therefore, let us consider the somewhat simpler (to describe) method involved in the use of the chain. The chain need not be composed of "half seed

[3] W.R. Bascom, *Ifa Divination* (Bloomington: Indiana University Press, 1969), p. 3.

shells," but can be made of cowries, of other kinds of wood, or of metal fashioned to represent seeds or, even, faces—perhaps of Ifa himself. Invariably these are arranged in a single chain composed of two halves of four units each. The length of chain separating the two halves is, reasonably enough, greater than that separating the units comprising each of the halves. The halves of four units each thus line up in corresponding pairs of units when the chain is grasped at its center. Further, the units themselves have both a figured and a plain side, either one of which may show upon the toss. When the babalawo casts the chain, each half has the possibility of falling into one of sixteen possible positions. All the figured surfaces may show, or all may be hidden, or the top unit may show its figure while the others hide theirs, and so on. When one takes the other half of the chain into account, it is clear that there the same number of variations exists. However, when one considers that for each position of the first half there are sixteen possible variations on the other, and that this is the case for each of the sixteen positions of that side, he sees that the possible number of configurations (odu) is the square of sixteen or 256.

For each of these 256 odu there is a number of verses. Let us consider for example that both halves of the chain, upon being cast, show all eight surfaces with the figured side up. This configuration is known as *ogbe ogbe*, or *ogbe meja* (twice *ogbe*) and Bascom provides twelve verses for it, only one of which might be applicable in the instance of a given act of divination, the apt one to be identified by the babalawo's client after the babalawo's recitation of all the relevant odu for that configuration.

The general outline of the procedure in divination is as follows. (1) The first cast is made to determine the figure for which the verses are recited. (2) Two casts are made to determine whether the prognostication is for good or for evil. (3) Five casts are made to find out what kind of good or evil is indicated. (4) A succession of double casts may be made to find out in more detail about the evil. (5) Two casts are made to find out whether a sacrifice ... is sufficient, or whether [an additional offering is required.] (6) If [this] is indicated, five casts are made to learn to whom it should be offered. (7) If [this] is to be made to a "white deity," it is identified by a succession of double casts. (8) Five casts are made to determine what is required as [this offering]. (9) If a live animal is required, a succession of double casts may be made to find out what kind. (10) The verses of the figure of the initial cast are recited, and the appropriate verse is selected. (11) The correct sacrifice is determined by a succession of double casts.[4]

In this extended process of either/or determinations, there is no evidence of synthetic dialectic. The process is one of forthright syndetic continuity.

The world of the Yoruba is a finitely discrete one. The gods are numbered; the realms of the universe are fixed, as is the progress of the spirits through them; categories of children are few and premised significantly upon the recurrence of souls; the notion of novelty, which is largely a function of the dialectical myth with its emphasis upon the synthesis, is difficult to conceive. Everything is subsumable under something else. Ifa divides the world into 256 categories of possible events—

[4] Ibid, p. 59.

or fewer, actually, since it is not the case that each odu is unique in either its specific demands or in its implications—and these are cut across by the denomination of five kinds of good and five kinds of evil.[5]

Observe how, in sacrifice, all possibilities are defined:

When an animal is sacrificed, its head is given to Eshu, but Ifa must be asked about the disposition of the body. The first question is whether it is to be eaten. If the answer is affirmative, the meat is cooked and eaten by the diviner and his family and visitors, the client receiving nothing. If the answer is negative, Ifa is asked whether it is to be given to another diviner and whether the diviner is an Elegan or an Olodu; finally, the names of individual diviners are suggested in sequence. If it is not to be given to a diviner, Ifa is asked if the meat is to be roasted and divided among the inhabitants of the diviner's compound. If the answer is negative, Ifa is asked whether it is to be cut up and put in a potsherd with palm oil and left as an offering ... for witches ... at a fork in the road, a river, and other specific places.[6]

The syndetic nature of this process is obvious, as well as are its continuity and its intension, which are to be seen in the narrowly defined categorical range of possibilities conceived for the disposition of the sacrifice. It is this rigorously preserved intension which defines the appositionality of the syndetic elements.

Those processes which are used to seek to bring the beneficent interventions of gods into the affairs of men also enact appositional syndetism in that they add to

[5] Ibid, p. 55.
[6] Ibid, p. 65.

that which is sacred to a god (an altar, a sculpture) those material conditions (the blood of an appropriate animal or some other appropriate food) which have been culturally defined to be the necessary and sufficient conditions of his presence or of acceptability to him. They are, in a special sense, the god's material synonyms, or similetic equivalents.

Appositional syndetism, intensive and continuous, is to be seen richly manifesting itself in other areas of Yoruba belief as well. In the concept of multiple souls for each individual; in the myth of the earth's founding, which has it that the earth was established from an aboriginal patch of earth which a cock scratched over the surface of the primordial waters; in the suggestion contained in the name of Ifa, the knower of fates, which actually means scraping, because he "scrapes" (fa) sickness and other evils away from those who are afflicted; in the Yoruba sense of ethnic identity deriving from kingdoms established by the sixteen sons of the culture hero, Oduduwo; and so forth. Incrementation has boundless aesthetic consequences, as we have already seen evidence for. But for good measure I throw in the wonder whether this is not the reason why it is that a sense of climax, as we perceive such a point—as the resolution of conflicts—is absent from much of the narrative, and perhaps from other forms as well. Is this owing to the fact that development tends to be additive rather than resolutional?

Appositional syndetism lies at the heart of the Yoruba conception of the generations, whose successiveness is such that the Yoruba families are thought to include both the dead and the unborn as well as the living. The importance of consecutivity is to be seen in the words for son, grandson, great-grandson—omo, omo omo, omo omo omo; and significantly in the round after round of the endless cycling of rebirth, emphasizing the close- ness of the additive terms—an inhibition upon range which, in the affecting presence, we recognize as inten- sion. Appositional syndetism as a mythic process, it would appear reasonable to assume, is as inevitable for the Yoruba to enact as polar continuity is for the European—in both conceptualization and presentation, so that syndetic intensive continuity becomes the para- mount metaphor of its achievement, especially since intension is so pronounced that it becomes a secondary or allusive metaphor to continuity itself. Continuity as the sheer realization and celebration of a significant feature of that very myth which makes the Yoruba culture Yoruba *must* be affecting. We have seen that this is so not under the circumstance of simple contem- plation or inspection, as the European would have it, but under the circumstance of its invocation as a viable and inexorable quantum in the universe of energy. It is, at the most fundamental point of consideration conceivable, through this profound incarnation of abso- lute myth that the Yoruba work becomes and endures *affecting.* The reason that the work is affecting, to put the matter somewhat differently, is organic with being Yoruba. The reason that it is a *presence*, a comple- mentary self to the witness, is that through the reality of metaphor it is the very embodiment of that myth which makes man conscious, it is the presentation, the viable principle of one's being. In the temporal forms, syndetic incrementation is to be seen, as we have ob- served previously, in that feature we have earlier referred to as the "atomistic achievement of continuity." We see it as well in the design executed on the surface of the Epa mask. But how is it to be seen in the sculptured forms themselves? Or more exactly, since we argue the existence of a system, how are the sculptured forms to be seen as incremental? There is no problem, to be sure, with those numerous sculpture which comprise groups of figures. The mere consecutivity of figures, to which narrative involvement is by no means necessary—and is indeed in most cases absent—is endowed with significance *only* in terms of the enactment of the myth-energy of incrementation.

Let us look for the purposes of a close pursuit of this question at a sheer, simple, and superb male figure (plate 20), instead of the Ogun axe or the Epa mask which we have already seen to be so rich with additive features. We may assume that this male had around the holding base upon which he stands multiple strings of cowrie shells, whose additivity is now as apparent to us as a cliché. Certain other instances of additivity are also clear; the fact that he holds objects; an axe in one hand and a bag or rattle in another; the fact that his face is scarred; the fact that he wears an intricately incised hat. But how is the form itself to be seen, the simple actuality of his body? If we *really look* at the piece, we perceive after a moment that its apparent simplicity, which is what first strikes us, is a masterpiece of understatement. The Yoruba love for the baroque is so great that even in such stringent works as this present one it accretes its presence. The body is as carefully formulated into its major masses, despite the differences in relative importance placed upon these masses, as were the works of the European Renaissance. Though subdued, each portion of the body clearly exists—feet, lower

legs, thighs, genitalia, abdomen, pectorals, neck, head—
features thereof—upper arms, lower arms, hands. It is
the sum of its parts. The back (plate 21), indisputably,
lacks the differentiation of the front, which argues
that—even though it is in the round—it was the artist's
intention that the piece should be seen from the front.
It is, in brief, absurd to conclude that an artist who
could so articulately conceive and execute the major
conformations of the ventral surface of the body could
not have been equally eloquent on the dorsal surface.
But it is the function of the back, syndetically, to be
the understated complement of the front. The Yoruba,
too, like subtlety.

We have now had the opportunity to apprehend the
mythoform of the Yoruba both in the fabric of their
social existence (part of what I shall finally call the
indicative mode of the myth) and in instances of the
affecting presence. It is therefore apparent that the
mythoform, perceived in the work of affecting presence,
does indeed inform and order the living of life. What
is true of the Yoruba is of course true of other peoples
as well. I have tried in the merest suggestion to indicate
how the mythoform infiltrates the fullness of the spectrum of European life as well, even though the analysis
provided was of a very ancient work—but, it must be
noted, a very ancient work that is singularly important
to us even today, one that was until very recent times
one of the most significant and believed faces of the
myth of polar continuity among large segments of the
European intelligentsia. It is safe to assume that this
time-tested "myth" will, perhaps toward some other end,
prove to be significant once again in the conduct of our
affairs. Such is the power of the mythoform of con-

sciousness when it is doubly presented, doubly celebrated as it is in the Oedipus.

At this penultimate point in our inquiry into the myth and the source of culture there are some generalizations that should be drawn concerning it. These generalizations have already been made at one point or another in the writing that has preceded, but it will be useful to draw them all together here.

1. The mythoform, being the myth upon which the consciousness is founded, is not, save in extraordinary circumstances, specifically and exoterically available to man.

2. The mythoform is the unquestioned and unquestionable basis of our perception, our beliefs, our values. Accordingly it owns great power.

3. The mythoform is prior to the bifurcation of our awareness into feeling and concept, prior to its bifurcation into time and space.

4. The mythoform informs all the people of a culture do and are. And the kinds of actions they commit are of several kinds, including simple exposition (the indicative mode of the myth) and celebration (the celebrative mode).

5. The affecting presence is a presence and is affecting *both* owing to the fact that it incarnates that myth which, most profoundly, we are. It shares with us the most basic principle of our humanity.

6. The mythoform always enacts itself in the structural and dynamic terms of the affecting presence. Sometimes it does so as well in the work's content.

7. Mythoforms of various cultures exist in specific spatio-temporal terms: extension or intension, continuity or discontinuity.

8. The mythoforms of more than one culture, obviously, may opt for the same disciplines; but this does not
mean that such cultures will necessarily have common
social or affecting forms.

9. Cultures that have apparently similar social and
affecting forms need not share the same mythoform.

The hypothesis of the cultural mythoform of consciousness, the founding of culture in consciousness with
an intransigent patterning to account for it, is a signal
advance which not only makes possible a humanistic
anthropology of significant promise but also stands in
good stead in terms of breathing a vigor and a renewed
pertinence into social anthropology. The understanding
of man as an experiencing agent, and this in a valuable
anthropological context, is thus possible.

But now the time has come to reconstitute forms from
the energy of myth through the completed spatial and
temporal works, so that, even if we cannot fully experience them as existential fields, we may yet *witness* them
as fully constituted from fundamental perceptions outward into the real works that are in their own existential
terms works in affecting presence.

So let us imagine that there is about incremental
intensive-continuity an unquestioned, though unformu-
lated, positive drive—a passion—concerning its desira-
bility, its inevitability indeed. Let us imagine that if
our belief were ever to be called into question we should
protest—reject alternatives, maintaining by the nature
of our insistence if not by articulated concept that it
and only it is the ultimate condition of the universe
and is therefore, in the most profound sense possible,
right. Let us acknowledge for our own part that we are
aware of what the affecting presence does, namely that

it incarnates this basic premise of our consciousness, and further that it does so in such a fashion that that very act of incarnation is at the same time a celebration, that it is brought about in inevitability, in belief, in passion, and in delight. Let us grant that as such it is a festivity or a sacrament in the very energy of being.

Let us further assume that incrementation can exist only under one circumstance, that of happening in a field of explicit energy—whether the field itself be spatial or temporal—and that this energy is of the force of growth, of the universe. This is the energy of the aesthetic, the cultural energy, as opposed to the energy of the work's fictive substance. It is, furthermore, the energy of appositional complementarity-in-continuity, rather than the energy of distillation with which the Western European is familiar as a result of perceiving the world ever as an endless pattern in the resolution of antimonies. Further, we must assume that that energy itself is greatly prized, even to the point of having been generalized to a critical position in the functioning of the universe and becoming both the mode and purpose of both the gods and men.

Let us grant that incrementation-in-energy can be incarnated into works of affecting presence by means of metaphors which are enacted in terms of intensive continuity—or intensivity in continuity, if we are to connote the quintessential role of energy, and that continuity in particular—disciplined in intensionality—is the unparalleled physical vessel in which that incarnation can occur.

Against a believed background of these presuppositions, then, let us perceive *Ogogoro Man in an Intoxicated Dream*. Behold! We see it now as a rich and

·

dramatic density of additives; fourteen figures existing
one with the other in relationships of balance through
complementarity, which is to be seen as a variation upon
mere seriation so that variety may be achieved and
additivity made both more interesting and more complex—this latter factor lending its own extra increment
of energy. Each of these figures comprises clearly defined
parts which are themselves additively profligate—and
all this against a background, and upon a foreground
of two similar contrapuntal motifs, intricately additive
within themselves, so that the foreground is additive
to the background, and vice versa. This, we understand,
achieves continuity atomistically—or as we now more
clearly see is the profound metaphor incarnating a
portion of the *charged* myth of the Yoruba consciousness. Finally, the intension exerted upon the
bodies, brought about by supplementary and complementary appositioning, and by the rigorous control of
the palette—all these reinforce that same dynamic of
continuity. If one can apprehend the work in all these
forms, instantaneously to be sure then he approaches
it as nearly as possible in the terms of breathless
incremental continuity in which it exists. *Ogogoro Man*
is a festivity in the Yoruba consciousness.

    And so it is also with *The Palm-Wine Drinkard*. Take
a profligacy of invention, of incredible scene heaped upon
incredible scene, yet each duplicating in some marvelous
variation the structure of others before and after it.
Endow this with friction against time brought about
by the dense rapidity of event, of chameleon transfor-
mations, of lavish baroqueness of scene and of action—all
this executed in careful complementarities and packed
into the fuse of its intensive-continuity. Now one begins

to perceive it in its rich energy of creative speed and seminal invention—a direct presentation of the mytho-form of incremental syndetic continuity! An energy reaction generating energy by celebrating it, celebrating energy by constituting it. Here exists being not only in the terms most fitting to it, but indeed in the only terms possible.

Why the affecting presence is a presence is now clear. It is a presence because it incarnates (as man incarnates) and is enflamed (as man himself is enflamed) with the very form-in-energy of human consciousness. Small wonder then that Joyce took as his challenge the task of forging within the smithy of his soul the consciousness of his race, choosing as his model the mighty artificer Daedalus. Small wonder that the myth of the maker whose creation bursts into life should remain viable, from ancient Greece's Pygmalion to Igor Stravinsky's Petrouchka. The affecting presence, and its creators—the best among them, at least—have known the secret and have tried to tell us.

This is awesomely the case in a pair of important brass pieces (plates 22, 23) from the Oro society of the Yoruba. These pieces are Elulu-Oro, the ultimate judge in this fatal society. They are made of metal, which means a base for the existence of the work which on the one hand requires the greatest energy of man and fire to produce and which on the other hand is ever prime because it is not subject to decay and the con-comitant loss of energy. Next the two pieces are elabo-rate, increasing element after element with the energy of incrementation. This is true not only in the three dimensions of their physical existence but in the fourth dimension of history as well, for we must presume that when they were viably in culture the two pieces were endowed in their presence with the energies of those awful judgments accountable to them.

The pieces are profoundly Yoruba, executing in the stylization of their bodies, in the idioms of hyperbole of the faces, the Yoruba imperatives carried to their ultimate realization. How else other than by achieving the essence of Yoruba-ism can one incarnate the awesome authority of these works? And they are as rich in the idioms of energy as they are in their incarnation of it, for the works not only are divine energy, they are equally presentative of energy in their aboutness—the mandalas surrounding the figures; the use of the human form as an instrument of detail, as is to be seen in the small figures, the topmost one seeming by compressed metaphor to be the generative phallus of the male, the other placed in the sacrificial cup upon the gravid abdomen of the basal female suggesting in profound ambiguity the inevitable and eternal circularity of association between birth and death—and perhaps re-birth as well; the chameleon, sometimes said to be symbolic of immortality, poised to enter the goddess' body, in ultimate impregnation. There is in this wholly presented, successfully *total* aboutness not only assent—to the order of the world—but awe-ful acquiescence to it as well. A fearful continuity and power are available. The rigorous physical infusion of the works is perfectly clear, as is the overall effectuation of the column. The myth of appositional syndetism, enacted in presentation along a brief continuum of awe, is asserted and assented to in mighty Presence!

We see in total, then, that the affecting presence is an existential field, richly alive with the electric structures and processes of consciousness, which with the believed power of myth quickens the affecting and conceptual dimensions into the presentation of being, brightly brought to focus upon—indeed infusing—the aboutness of the work and delivering it into living particularity, aboutness into brought-aboutness. The affecting presence which so exists glows with the radiant tension between those two orders inextricably joined within it—mythoform and myth, culture and particularity, consciousness and immedia, affect and metaphor. The affecting presence is the presence of man in his uniqueness subtly creating the world in his own image, his interiority's eloquent emissary to the world at large. Who would understand man must first understand his externalized and living fixity.

But it is to the understanding of the cultural myth and source, the wellspring of culture, that this book is devoted. The affecting presence is only a means to this end, most useful of all of man's acts because it alone presents the cultural myth in its own terms, enacting and celebrating them in structure, in dynamics, and in substance. But the myth suffuses all of each culture, sharply in those cultures which have long history and have retained a vigorous homogeneity; obscurely, perhaps in those which are everchanging concoctions of invented, begged, borrowed, or stolen novelty.

The synthetic myth is a dialectical one. Its concern is with "truth" which it acknowledges is evolutionary and relative, so that one truth is opposed by a subsequent alternative from which confrontations some kind of synthesis is reached. This process is never-ending and in a frivolous age when alternatives are perhaps less clear or less weighty than at other times, genuine dialectical process is replaced by its shoddy step-cousin which is called *game*. Instead of being driven to ever more relevant syntheses, under such circumstances people become content—indeed enraptured—with mere novelty. It is either synthesis or novelty which, in art, drives the synthetic culture from school to successive school—from, as it were, new allophone to new allophone of cultural ambient which is the key mode of the work's existence.

The syndetic myth on the other hand is not specifically dedicated either to the proposition that truth is evolutionary or, for that matter, to the proposition that the achievement of truth is a desirable cultural goal. The search for truth consumes Ahab; the Tiv reject the terms of this consideration. The syndetic culture is an additive culture, premised not upon truth but—among the Yoruba at least—upon power. Thus instead of constant dialectical striving for alloforms of cultural space—or for mere novelty—the syndetic culture repeats well-known forms. The imperative of the synthetic culture is evolutionary, logical change; of the syndetic culture the imperative is incrementation ... in traditional Yorubaland, at least, this imperative is under the auspices of the dominant of stability, or the minimization of change. Thus does Yoruba culture produce innumerable works in a limited number of types, most of whose members bear strikingly close relationships one to another. Both synthetic and syndetic cultures share a common external characteristic: each by its nature is necessarily committed to a marked level of production of works of affecting presence if its myth is to be enacted—the one because the achievement of novelty or of significant synthesis must ever be enacted; and the other because its repeated enactment is a philosophical necessity. These myths lie deeply in our tropal consciousness, prior to all subsequent distinctions—as I have previously pointed out—into time and space, concept and affect, symbol and presentation, form and process. And yet all these subsequent refractions of the myth into terms of intension or extension, of continuity or discontinuity enact it. I have called the spatio-temporal dimensions of a work's existence its *discipline*, or more precisely I have used the term to describe the spatio-temporal uses of a culture. Now we may see them as the discipline of the consciousness breathed with humanity by the cultural myth which founds it.

But the myth exists in modes as well as in disciplines, and these may be called the *indicative*, which is the mode of living one's life, and the mode in which we "objectively" and analytically engage with the world; the *subjunctive*, which is the mode of possession, prophecy, and divination; the *imperative*, which is the mode of the enactment of myth in morality and law; the *celebrative*, which is the presentational mode, the mode of the object or the event of affecting presence; and the *conceptual* mode. Because of my special orientation we have discovered more about the celebrative mode than any other. Notably we have discovered why it is that the affecting presence is both affecting and a presence. It is affecting because it is impossible to present the conditions of one's consciousness without inherent affect; and a presence because the myth of our being is our most basic vital principle. It is the seed of our *human* existence. The European aesthetic of beauty and truth, and the Yoruba aesthetic of energy and process are the strategems under which the cultural myth is livingly incarnated. Both assert and assent to their myths. Indeed assent is a significant part of the celebrative mode. *A Prison Scene* asserts a dialectic, fearfully assenting. This is not to say that Goya assents to the conditions of the prisoners. Quite the contrary is eloquently the case. But his assent to the mythoform, superbly, affords the dynamics for the great irony which is the basis for the specific dialectic of the work, that one between the oppressors and the oppressed, between darkness and light, between closure and openness.

The cultural mythoform is the existential imperative of all those human beings who constitute it. Discernable in only the thinnest of outline, at the present at least, it is largely ineffable. But the fact that it is not fully perceived does not diminish its progenerative power. Perhaps the myth is even enhanced by its obscurity. Whatever the case, it is clear that the future of a humanistic anthropology must in considerable measure be dedicated to the revelation and the appreciation of the cultural myth.

Index

151